MORE
than an
AVERAGE
GUY

The Story of
LARRY PATTON

By
JANET KASTNER

With Afterword
JOSH McDOWELL

DARING PUBLISHING GROUP, INC.
LIFE ENRICHMENT PUBLISHERS • DARING BOOKS
CANTON • OHIO

Cover design by David Riley

Published by Life Enrichment Publishers
P.O. Box 20050, Canton, Ohio 44701

Printed in the United States of America.

Library of Congress Cataloging-in-Publication Data

More than an average guy : the story of Larry Patton /
by Janet Kastner.
   p.   cm.
Includes index.
ISBN 0-938736-25-6
   1. Patton, Larry--Health. 2. Cerebral palsy-- Patients
--United States--Biography. I. Title.
RC388.P37K37   1989
362.1 '96836 '0092--dc20
[B]   89-1447
                                   CIP

Dedication

From Larry:
To Steve, my brother, for all the love and support
over the years and for being my life-long best friend,

and

From Janet:
To parents and families of handicapped children.
Take courage.

Table of Contents

Acknowledgments

We wish to thank the following persons for their help in the process of writing this book. Their aid was invaluable to us and much appreciated.

Mary and Jim Wall, Marsha Snider, Terri Harding, Eunice and Howard Bitzer, Craig Davies, Voris Conrad, IBM, Jim Rafferty, Mary Kirkwood, Charles Jones, Barbara Kerby, James Langdal, Janice Finn, Nancy Bagnall, Chris Gram, Bonnie Giffin, Harry Patton family, Steve and Libby Weber, Josh McDowell, Bob Tiede, Detroit Institute for Children, Terry Vaughn, Steve Hull, John Mitchell family, John Hevel family, Jimmye Sue Lickliter, Jeni and Dick Wiggers, John Burg, Mark Keegan, Don Kastner, Elaine Wright Colvin, Pauline Grimes, Tilford and Maxine Largent, Dwight and Mildred Lane, Ken and Marian LaRowe, Judi Geithman, and Elton Trueblood.

In addition, there were countless prayers said on behalf of this endeavor, that the book would truly be what God wanted and that He might use it to His glory. We thank all those who upheld us in this way.

1

Wait and See

"Please, God, let my baby live!"

Under the hot light of the delivery room, Sue waited. The sheet over her knees hid the unfamiliar doctor and the solitary registered nurse. Terse instructions and muttered comments came from them, but no cry from the baby. Although numb from the saddle block and exhausted from the difficult birth, Sue was fully conscious.

"Mrs. Patton, we're having a little trouble getting him to breathe. Nurse, let's try . . ."

Sensing the need for silence, Sue asked no questions but redoubled her silent prayer, "Please, God, let my baby live!" *Why didn't my doctor tell me she was going to California?* Sue asked herself. The hospital had told them when Bill brought Sue in for delivery that night. Now here was Dr. Shuck, a stranger to the Pattons.

This was their first child. The pregnancy had been a normal one. The birth was not. The umbilical cord was wrapped so many times and so tightly around the baby's neck that it had prevented his movement down the birth canal. Dr. Shuck ordered a saddle block instead of a general anesthetic. Sue had protested, but Dr. Shuck brusquely told her he would make decisions like that. Now she was acutely aware of the struggle going on for the baby's life.

The hands on the delivery room clock moved

inexorably—1:45, 1:50, 1:55. "Please, God, let my baby live!"

Dr. Shuck and one nurse were the only staff members on that floor of the hospital that night. There were no LPN's or nurses' aides, or orderlies or student nurses . . .

"Nurse, get the . . ." The words were lost to Sue. "It should be over there."

The nurse looked, but the piece was missing. She couldn't call anyone else to look.

The doctor had to improvise. In desperation, he said, "Fill that pan with cold water. I'm going to submerge him. Maybe the shock will make him gasp and expand his lungs."

2:00.

2:05.

Dr. Shuck massaged the baby gently with towels, trying everything he could think of to get this baby breathing.

"Please, God . . ."

And then, at 2:10 A.M., Larry William Patton finally was able to breathe on his own. It was January 11, 1956.

The nurse washed the infant and then hurried off to put him in an incubator. At nine pounds twelve ounces, he looked like a giant next to the preemies in the other glass cases.

Satisfied, the doctor finished the delivery and turned his attention to Sue, cleaning up. "I've never worked so long on a baby and had him live," he told her. "I worked longer than this on my own child, but he died. I'll tell you one thing, your own doctor would have given you ether, and then your baby wouldn't have had a chance. There is a possibility that your boy may have cerebral palsy. I'm not sure how much oxygen he lost."

"What's cerebral palsy?"

"Well, lack of oxygen to the brain can cause some problems, you know. Don't say anything to your husband about it at this point," he cautioned her.

Why can't I tell Bill? Sue wondered, but she was too tired and too inexperienced to ask any more questions.

It was well after three A.M. when Dr. Shuck found Bill in the fathers' waiting room. "You have a son," he reported. "There was a breathing problem at first. We put him in an incubator, and he's doing fine now. Sue is resting. Why not go on home and come back and see her later?"

Bill thanked him and went back to their tiny mobile home behind the Women's Gymnasium on the campus of Hanover College. Nothing had been said about the difficult birth or the possibility of cerebral palsy.

Several hours later, baby Larry was brought to his mother's bed for the first time. There were red rings around his neck from the umbilical cord. Those rings would be visible for many weeks.

The next day, Jimmye Sue Lickliter, a neighbor and good friend from the small cluster of trailers, came to the hospital to visit. On her way to Sue's room, she passed the nursery and looked in at the rows of cribs. In the center were the incubators, and among the pitifully small pre-mature babies was a robust infant whose head seemed to touch one end of the bed and his feet the other. The name card said Larry William Patton. *Why is he in an incubator?* she wondered, all kinds of fears springing to her mind.

She hurried down the hall to Sue's room and gently pushed the door open. Like her baby's, Sue's body nearly filled the bed. Tall, big-boned, athletic, she seemed built to give birth easily. *What went wrong?* Jimmye Sue worried.

"Hi, Susie! I took a peek at the baby on my way to your room. You really had a big one, didn't you! How're you doin'?"

Sue's face lit with pleasure and an odd light of hope. Jimmye Sue had a little boy herself. Maybe she could tell Sue more than Dr. Shuck had. He had said not to tell Bill about the possibility of Larry's having cerebral palsy, but he hadn't said, "Don't tell anyone." Here was her chance.

"It was really rough. I've never been so scared in my life!" Sue went on to describe the delivery in detail and finished, "Do you know anything about cerebral palsy? And can you figure out why I shouldn't tell Bill about it?"

"No, I don't know a thing about that cerebral palsy, but probably he doesn't want you to say anything to Bill because he's in the middle of final exam week. I guess Dr. Shuck doesn't think it's enough of a problem to worry him with now."

Jimmye Sue invented that excuse to soothe Sue, but inside she was furious. What a cruel thing to tell a new mother and then not let her share it with her husband! This was too big a burden for Sue to carry alone. Jimmye Sue tried again to cheer her friend. "He looks fine and healthy. Have you fed him yet?"

"I tried, but he couldn't nurse. He seemed too weak. Did you see the red rings around his neck from the cord?"

"No, he's all wrapped up in a cuddly blanket. He looks so sweet. Listen, I've got to get on home. When the doctor comes in, you ask him all your questions. I'm sure everything is going to be all right. Bill sends his love. He'll be in this afternoon."

"Okay. Thanks for coming. We'll be home in a few days."

Jimmye Sue's visit had helped, but Sue's fears were growing with every passing hour. Dr. Shuck came in, busily assured her that the baby was fine and so was she, and bustled off before she could ask her questions.

Bill came later that afternoon, strong, solid, reassuring. He smiled shyly, kissed Sue, and gave her some roses. "Looks like you've lost some weight," he joked.

Sue clung to him for a minute, then wiped some tears from the corners of her eyes. "Have you seen Larry yet?"

"Just through the window in the nursery. How's he doing?"

"Fine, I guess. Did you see the red marks on his neck from the umbilical cord?"

"No, I didn't notice. I guess they'll go away before long."

A strained silence fell between them. Sue had a secret, and Bill didn't know how to talk to a woman who had just given birth, even if she was his wife. Finally they spoke simultaneously.

"How was your final today?"

"Dutch's final was awful!"

They laughed, and then another silence. Finally Bill said, "Well, I've got another final tomorrow to study for. If you don't mind, I'd better get on back and hit the books. You sure you're okay?"

"Yeah, I'm okay. You go on and study. Will you come back tomorrow?"

"Sure. Anything you need?"

So many chances to tell him what was uppermost in her mind, but Sue bottled it up. "I guess not. Thanks for the flowers. They sure are beautiful. Must have cost a lot."

Bill grinned. "Well, it's not every day a man has his first son. You rest now. See you tomorrow."

As he walked out, Sue turned away, clutched the sheets desperately, and clenched her teeth against the lonely anxiety.

The following day, Bruce Gannaway came. He was the pastor of the Hanover Presbyterian Church, where Bill and Sue were members. By then, Larry still had not been able to nurse, and the red rings were no fainter. Sue's fears had reached terrifying proportions. She confided in her pastor, and with compassion he immediately arranged for Dr. Shuck to talk to Sue and Bill together about their baby.

On January 13, two days after Larry's birth, two days of confusion, tension, and terror for Sue, the consultation with the doctor finally took place.

"Because it took so long for the baby to be able to breathe on his own, his brain may not have received all the oxygen it needed during those twenty-five minutes. Lack of oxygen to the brain can cause cerebral palsy in varying degrees of severity. Just keep an eye on him as he develops. If nobody has diagnosed cerebral palsy by the time he's two years old, he probably won't have it," Dr. Shuck said.

They still didn't know anything. They didn't know what to watch for as Larry developed or what doctors to take him to. But there is something about a medical manner that makes people think they are getting answers when in fact they are not. Sue and Bill felt reassured and asked no questions. The next two years presented no immediate problems. They could take their baby home and expect that everything would be all right.

Dr. Shuck's final word to them was ominous, though. "If you find he does have cerebral palsy, I'd advise you to put him in an institution and forget you ever had him."

After the doctor left, Bill's usually impassive face changed. His jaw was set, and his eyes glinted. "It makes me mad that he told you and not me about this cerebral palsy possibility. You've been through enough with the delivery. He should have told me!"

But what was done was done. Only Sue heard what Bill had to say about that. He didn't tell Dr. Shuck what he thought.

A few days later, Bill brought his family home. Before long, the steam of the bottle sterilizer and the rising heat from the electric heater made their trailer a capsule of warmth in the bitter January cold. "Shut the door quick!" was the welcome for each of the campus friends who came to see the new baby nestled in the bassinet just inside the door.

Everyone exclaimed about how big Larry was. In fact, before his birth there had been several bets among Bill's fraternity brothers that Sue was carrying twins. Besides the red rings around Larry's neck, the only other noticeable physical defect was that his right foot bent upward from the ankle toward the shin.

When Larry was about one month old, Bill and Sue took
him to visit her parents, Jim and Mary Wall, in Winchester,
Indiana. Mr. Wall was in poor health, so Bill and Sue agreed
not to worry her parents by mentioning the possibility of the
baby's cerebral palsy. However, during that week's visit, Larry
caught a cold. Sue took him to the Walls' family physician,
Dr. Painter. As he examined the baby, Sue said, "When Larry
was born, the cord was wrapped around his neck so much
that the doctor couldn't get him to breathe for about 25
minutes. He said Larry might have cerebral palsy. What do
you think? Does he have it?"

Dr. Painter continued examining Larry and without looking up replied, "You can only wait and see."

Back at Hanover, Dr. Shuck continued to care for Larry.
When the baby suffered with diarrhea for quite a while, Dr.
Shuck suggested a pediatrician in Louisville see him.

Sue took that opportunity, too, to explain Larry's birth and
ask about cerebral palsy. The pediatrician merely said it was
too soon to tell and recommended taking Larry off milk to
cure the diarrhea.

Dr. Shuck advised them not to worry about Larry's foot.
In his opinion it would probably be all right. Sue's parents,
however, were not satisfied to have Bill and Sue accept that
answer. They urged them to take Larry to Dr. Garceau, an
orthopedic physician in Indianapolis, who had treated their
nephew's club feet.

When they took Larry to this fourth doctor, Sue again
related the birth story. Dr. Garceau, like the others, said, "Too
soon to tell. But let's put a brace on this foot for six weeks
and see if we can strengthen it without surgery."

A smooth plaster brace extending from mid-calf to instep
was fitted over the front of Larry's leg and held in place with
tape. The Pattons went home to wait and see.

During the next few months, they did not go from doctor

to doctor trying to find someone to confirm or deny the possibility of cerebral palsy. They couldn't afford to financially, and perhaps they couldn't afford to emotionally either. They did not even try to learn as much as they could about CP. They weren't trying to avoid facing the possibility that Larry might be handicapped. They had asked several doctors, and all had said, "It's too early to tell. Just wait and watch his development." And he was developing. He was a healthy, bright-eyed boy. After the diarrhea stopped, he gained weight slowly but steadily. He held his head up when placed on his abdomen at five weeks. He laughed aloud at 18 weeks. He began rolling over at four months and reached for toys about a month later.

So theirs wasn't just an attitude of "If we don't look, maybe it will go away." Both Bill and Sue were very busy—Bill as a full-time student working a couple of part-time jobs, and Sue as a full-time mother also working part-time doing typing at home to bring in a little extra income. Their social life consisted of attending college athletic events and church functions and playing cards with campus friends. Almost always, Larry went along. A babysitter was a luxury the Pattons couldn't afford.

School, sports, church, and part-time jobs: these were permanent aspects of Bill and Sue's life together. In fact, the pattern had been established from their early teenage years. Both were industrious, resourceful, busy people, not given to much introspection and not having time to agonize over uncertainties. They loved their baby and wanted to believe he would be all right.

Yet others were aware very early that Larry was not developing normally. Jimmye Sue next door kept a close eye on Larry while keeping her fears from Sue and Bill. Sue's parents were convinced by the time Larry was six months old that something was wrong, but because Sue and Bill hadn't mentioned any problem, Mr. and Mrs. Wall asked no questions.

By seven months, Larry still wasn't sitting up alone. When Sue went to Dr. Pratt for her own medical reasons, she took Larry along and asked the doctor to check him, too. Dr. Pratt said Larry was a fine healthy baby and was probably slow in developing coordination because of his size. After all, he did weigh a little over 19 pounds.

When Sue and Larry returned from that office visit, Jimmye Sue was waiting in the doorway of her trailer to hear what the doctor had said.

"He's fine," Sue reported. "Dr. Pratt says he's just slow because he's so big." She herself was reassured and proud of her big baby.

"That's great," Jimmye Sue replied, her smile reflecting Sue's beaming grin. But that night she said to her husband, "Arlan, I don't care what the doctor said—I *know* there's something wrong with that baby! He's not *that* big for his age any more."

"Yeah, I think so, too, but we can't say anything to Sue and Bill. They've done all they can. After Bill graduates and they get settled somewhere, somebody'll find out what it is and know what to do about it."

Bill's last semester at Hanover was the fall of 1956. He was a physical education major, and in Indiana in the '50's that meant he wanted a job as a high school basketball coach. He had played varsity basketball as a high school senior. As a college senior, he coached the collegiate freshman team. But there were no mid-term coaching positions open in Indiana that year.

Finishing up the requirements for his major, Bill took a course in teaching drivers' training and something called Adaptive Physical Education. These two classes turned out to be more significant for the future than all the classes in basketball. He wrote a paper for Adaptive P. E. on designing an exercise program for someone with a foot problem like Larry's, to strengthen the muscles and enable him to participate in recreational sports. It was the beginning of an attitude that said, "Take what you've got and see how much you can make of it. Don't waste time on what you don't have."

Meanwhile, Sue's mother, Mary Wall, was taking classes at Ball State University. One evening when the weather was particularly bad, her husband, Jim, drove Mary to the campus and studied the bulletin board in the education building while he waited for her class to end. He noticed that Highland Park High School in the Detroit area was advertising for a drivers' training teacher. Because of a personal friendship between the president of Ball State and the school superintendent in Highland Park, job opportunities available there were advertised at Ball State and not at Hanover. Jim Wall copied the information, and when they got home that night, he phoned Bill.

Since there were no openings for basketball coaches, and since he needed a job immediately at the beginning of second semester, Bill applied for the drivers' training opening. He didn't think his chances were very good, but Sue reassured him.

"I'm sure you'll get it. A clean-cut, All-American boy, a veteran, a father, of course they'll hire you."

And they did. Later the Pattons could see God's hand had been at work. It must have been more than coincidence that the weather had been bad enough for Jim Wall to drive Mary to class, have time to study the bulletin board, notice an announcement that Bill would never have known about otherwise, and give him the needed information.

It was January, 1957. Larry was one year old and still could not sit alone or pull up. He still had the random, uncontrolled movements of a six-month old baby. The foot had straightened without surgery, and Dr. Garceau thought Larry would be able to walk normally.

Moving to the Detroit area was exciting. Although they had been self-supporting and had put down roots at Hanover, they had always known their life there was temporary. Royal Oak, Michigan, was very much the real, adult world. Their first floor, one-bedroom furnished apartment felt spacious compared to the trailer. Bill's salary of $4200 seemed enormous compared to the $2700 Sue had earned when she taught business education the year before Larry's birth.

The First Presbyterian Church in Royal Oak was only a couple of blocks from their apartment. Bill's boss, who was a member there, invited them to attend. The pastor called on them and asked if they would like to join. It was a large, wealthy, suburban church enjoying the religious boom of the mid-fifties—very different from the small, tradition-bound, town-and-gown church at Hanover. It was a whole new life in Royal Oak. Because of their upbringing, Sue and Bill expected the church to be a big part of it. They joined, without "shopping around."

"Listen," the clerk of session told them, "we're a big congregation. You can be as involved as you want to be, or you can get lost in the crowd. If you want to be active, speak up and we'll put you to work. Otherwise, you might not get asked."

So Bill began to usher on Sunday mornings. Sue joined the Women's Association and became a circle member. They joined a couple's group, and they went to church dinners at least once a month.

Outside the church, they formed a pinochle club with three other couples. Bill's job entitled them to free passes to all the athletic events at his school, so they took Larry along and went to ball games. They quickly made friends with their neighbors in the apartment building. It was an exciting new life.

But it didn't take long to realize that Bill's salary was very low for the average in that area. The Pattons were surrounded by wealth at church, yet they could barely make ends meet. Sue didn't have opportunities for part-time jobs as she had in Hanover. And by the end of March, they knew she was pregnant again.

Larry had been progressing slowly. By this time he could sit up alone and could stand while holding onto something. He was doing better at holding his head erect, although it usually ducked to one side.

Two pieces of equipment were helpful, a play- and feeding-table with a seat recessed in the center, and a Taylor Tot with the long push handle removed from the back. Strapped into the seat of the play table, he could reach for toys or bits of food and entertain himself. The Taylor Tot became his walker as he pushed himself energetically around the apartment. The rubber-encased bumpers protected the furniture. He was curious, mischievous, and cute, but he wasn't talking, walking, or feeding himself. Still, no doctor had said that he had cerebral palsy, or that he didn't.

Sue asked friends at church to recommend a gynecologist, and they suggested Dr. Kohler, one of four OB/GYN doctors practicing together. The first time she met Dr. Kohler, Sue told him about Larry's birth. Dr. Kohler assured her there was no reason for a similar delivery this time.

During the course of the pregnancy, she met all four doctors, and she felt they were careful and dependable. Yet she worried. Would this baby be like Larry? Would the delivery go all right? Was there something in her physical make-up that would always produce babies like . . . babies with problems?

After each appointment, the examining physician reassured her that everything was fine. She walked out on a cloud of relief. But by the next appointment, that cloud was one of apprehension over her head.

Late in the summer of 1957, Larry caught a cold. After asking church friends for a recommendation again, Sue took him to Wake Pediatric Clinic. The doctor on duty happened to be Dr. Michael Sheridan, a noted diagnostician. After checking Larry, he said, "I believe he may have a mild form of cerebral palsy. I want you to take him to the Detroit Orthopaedic Clinic for evaluation and recommendation. They'll be able to tell you for sure. It may take a few weeks to get an appointment."

A letter telling the Pattons to come on a specific date must have been lost in the mail. D.O.C. phoned to see why they had not kept the appointment, and a new date was set: December 12, 1957.

A month before that appointment, on November 10, Bill took Sue to Women's Hospital in Detroit for the birth of their second child. Once again there were changes in plans at the last minute. Sue had toured the hospital where her doctor had planned to deliver the baby, but when Bill phoned him to say the labor pains had started, he learned that that hospital was full. They were to go to Women's Hospital. Last time a different doctor, this time a different hospital. What else would go wrong?

Dr. Kohler met Sue in the delivery room. Her pains were excruciating, and the baby wouldn't come. Finally the doctor said, "It's a breach birth, Mrs. Patton. I'm going to give you a spinal."

"Thank you," she sighed. With the pain relieved, finally she gave birth to Steven James, ten pounds.

Dr. Kohler pronounced the baby healthy and whole. Sue brushed tears from her eyes as she held her second son for a moment before he was taken to the nursery. *Is there such a thing as a normal birth?* she wondered, exhausted.

The contrast between Women's Hospital in Detroit and the hospital where Larry had been born was striking. Women's was so much bigger, more modern, better staffed and equipped. Sue couldn't help wondering what a difference there might have been if Larry had been born here. She wrestled with resentment, regret, and pain. She thought, maybe for the first time, of a malpractice suit.

But then her upbringing and her basic practical nature came through. "You can't go back," she told herself. "Larry is 22 months old, and Dr. Shuck did get him to breathe." Jim and Mary Wall had taught her well: take the circumstances of life and deal with them in the best way possible. Thank God, Steve was fine.

On December 12, 1957, Bill and Sue took Larry down Woodward Avenue into the heart of the city to the Detroit Orthopaedic Clinic. At that time, it was using an old residence for its quarters. It looked dingy and decrepit in the cold rain that gloomy winter day.

"If it hasn't been diagnosed by the time he's two, he probably doesn't have it," Dr. Shuck had said. Here it was just one month before his second birthday. They were finally about to know. In spite of their parental pride that wanted to deny there was anything wrong, deep down they knew Larry's development was more than slow. It was time to identify the problem.

Inside the clinic, bright colors, cheerful people, and an optimistic bustling attitude raised their spirits. Larry was examined by a physical therapist, an occupational therapist, and a speech therapist.

"Is this Larry Patton?" the physical therapist asked the child.

"Yes, it is," Sue answered for him, because Larry's three word vocabulary didn't include his own name.

A social worker was assigned to the Pattons. She told them about the services offered at the Clinic, including a mother's group which met weekly. Sue would be expected to attend if Larry were accepted as a patient and enrolled in the nursery school.

No diagnosis was made that day. A second appointment and conference were set for December 18 with an orthopedic doctor.

The following week, Bill and Sue were overwhelmed to see many people present as Dr. Walsh examined Larry. The Detroit Orthopaedic Clinic is also a teaching center for Wayne Medical School and Wayne State's School of Social Work. There were interns, therapists, and student social workers observing and taking notes.

"Are you Larry Patton?" Dr. Walsh asked him.

"Yes, he is," Sue answered, as she had the week before.

"Do not answer his questions for him!" Dr. Walsh snapped. "I was talking to *Larry*."

Hurt and embarrassed, Sue bit her lip to keep from making a defensive answer. She struggled to keep her composure until she could leave the room. Then she burst into tears. She had answered for Larry last week and no one had told her not to. After all, the child couldn't even talk yet! How could he answer for himself? And for Dr. Walsh to snap at her in front of all those strangers! How cruel!

Yet, it was a valuable lesson. If she spoke for him, Larry wouldn't *have* to learn to speak for himself. He must be encouraged to do anything and everything he could for himself. Sue and Bill had to learn to let him try and try again without assistance. They must caution others not to help him, too.

After the examination, Dr. Walsh told the Pattons, and the room full of observing professionals, that Larry had a mild form of athetoid cerebral palsy. He had movements which he could not control because there were interruptions from his brain to whatever part of his body he was trying to move. His motions were smooth and flowing, not jerky like those of the spastic cerebral palsied. All his extremities were affected: his legs, his arms, his head. His speech was also involved. A cerebral palsied person is not necessarily mentally retarded, although that part of the brain is sometimes affected. In Larry's case, that was not a problem. His intelligence was at least average and possibly higher than that.

"Will he be able to support himself as an adult?" Bill and Sue wanted to know.

"We don't know at this point what his full potential will be. Through therapy here at the Clinic and exercises at home, we'll be able to develop his capabilities to their upper limit, whatever that turns out to be. Because we are a United Fund agency, our fee is based on whatever the family can afford to pay. We'd like you to submit a financial statement every six months. Our bookkeeper will give you the forms to fill out. Here are several pamphlets about the Clinic and about CP. Take them home. Study them. Whatever questions you have, we'll be glad to try to answer. With the holidays coming up, let's make your next visit January 9th. Then you can get started with the physical therapist."

As they drove back out Woodward Avenue that afternoon, Bill and Sue were silent, each absorbed in thought. Larry bobbed around, strapped in his car seat between them.

Keeping his eyes on the traffic, Bill asked himself, *Will Sue be able to handle this? She's led such a protected life. Is she strong enough to care for a handicapped child? How can we possibly afford to care for him? Will he ever be able to support himself, or will we be saddled with him forever?*

And Sue, looking straight ahead, twisted her fingers and thought, *Is this hereditary? What will our families think? How much help will they be, or will they be part of the problem? What will it be like for Steve to grow up with a handicapped brother?* And the most frightening question of all, *Will Bill still love us? Will he stand by me and support me, or will this disappointment kill something inside him?*

Deep down, both of them were thinking, *What have we done to deserve this? What kind of God lets this happen?*

Larry's head brushed against Sue's shoulder and his left hand touched Bill's arm. Instinctively they turned to him, and their eyes met. From deep within each of them came a smile of love and encouragement.

"Do you remember what Dr. Shuck said?" Bill asked.

"I'll never forget. 'If you find he does have CP, my advice is to put him in an institution and forget you ever had him.'"

"At least there's no question of *that*. Help is available. His capabilities are an unknown factor, but whatever they are, he is our child, and we will help him achieve his full potential. Right?"

"Right," Sue agreed, drawing a deep breath of relief and bracing herself for whatever the future would be.

2

The Network Begins

Ruth Foster sipped the coffee Sue had poured. She was the chairman of Sue's circle of the Women's Association at church and a close friend. Baby Steven lay sleeping on Ruth's lap. Through the curl of steam rising from the cup, she asked, "Just what is cerebral palsy anyway?"

Sue had been studying the pamphlets from D.O.C., so she was ready for the question. "Because it took Larry so long to breathe on his own at birth, some of the brain cells died from lack of oxygen. These dead cells cause an interruption from the brain to whatever part of his body he's trying to move. You know how all muscles work in pairs, in opposition to each other?"

"No, I didn't know that."

"Sure. When you flex your arm to show your biceps . . ." Sue demonstrated, "this bulge on the top is a contracted muscle. What allows it to contract is the triceps, this extended muscle below the bone." She ran the back of her index finger along the smooth underside of her upper arm. "These two muscles counter-balance each other. When one contracts, its partner expands, like a see-saw. All the muscles in the body work that way."

"Thanks, teach!" Ruth grinned. "Now what happens in Larry's case?"

Sue pushed her glasses back up her nose and continued.

"In Larry's case, the interruption from the brain keeps certain pairs from working like that. The counter-balancing force has been destroyed, so the remaining part over-acts. That's why he has all these random motions."

"Oh, now I understand. Can anything be done about it?"

Larry lurched around the living room in his Taylor Tot, deliberately bumping Ruth's leg and then grinning mischievously when he had her attention. She gave him an affectionate squeeze and sent him giggling and spinning across the room.

Sue chided him automatically, "Stop it, Larry. Don't be a pest." Then she continued with enthusiasm, "Detroit Orthopaedic Clinic has a fantastic program. They want us to bring him down there three times a week to work with a physical therapist, an occupational therapist, and a speech therapist. They've assigned a case worker to us, and there's a mother's group that meets once a week that I'm required to attend."

"Great! And what will all this do for Larry?"

"They'll teach him to control these random movements and eventually to walk and dress and feed himself. They'll help him learn to speak."

"Oh, Sue! That's wonderful! What a blessing that this kind of help is available! But it must be terribly expensive."

"That's the other good news. It's a United Fund agency, so they charge us only what we can afford to pay. On Bill's salary, that certainly won't be very much! We have to turn in a financial statement every six months."

"Everything seems to have been taken care of, then."

"Yeah, well," Sue said hesitantly, "the only thing is, I don't know how we're going to get him down to the D.O.C. three times a week. Bill has to drive to work, and we certainly can't afford a second car. And I don't know what I'm going to do with Steve. I would hate to drag him along, but I can't afford a babysitter. All this wonderful help available for Larry, just what he needs, but I don't know how we can take advantage of it."

"I see what you mean," Ruth agreed. She set aside her empty coffee cup and snuggled Steve, cherishing the feel of his downy head against her neck. "Are you coming to our Women's Association Christmas tea tomorrow afternoon?"

"No, I have to meet Bill at school for something going on there. I'll try to get to the meeting next month."

"Okay. I'll call you in a couple of days. I have to run now." She reluctantly laid the baby on the couch. "Bye, Larry," Ruth called, slipping into her coat. Then at the door she turned again. "Sue, don't worry. It'll work out. You'll see."

"I hope you're right. Thanks for coming over." Sue forced a smile as her friend left. Then leaning against the closed door, she faced her suddenly crying infant. The imp in the Taylor Tot banged into her leg and gave her a lop-sided grin. "I hope she's right," Sue muttered doggedly. "Larry, did you make Steve cry?"

Two days later Ruth returned, triumphantly waving a paper. "At the Association meeting at church yesterday, I told the women about your problem of getting Larry into the city three times a week. It's all taken care of. We even have substitutes lined up just in case someone can't make it."

Sue sank into the nearest chair, speechless. She studied the list. "I don't even know most of these women!"

"You will!" Ruth laughed. "Here you have all these new friends. You ride along on the days the mothers' group meets, and the rest of the time you can send Larry and stay home with Steve."

"I just don't know what to say! We can never repay all these people!"

"You don't have to. They're happy to give Larry their time, knowing he'll get the help he needs."

Good manners struggled with false pride. *We're a charity project*, she thought. *But if I refuse, I'll hurt all these kind people, and I really can't see any other way to get Larry down there.*

"Thank you," she said finally. "How can I thank *them*?" She cocked an eyebrow toward the schedule.

"Just keep them informed about Larry's progress. That's all the thanks they'll want."

"You found a way," Sue said. "I'll *never* forget this."

Ruth just smiled quietly.

3

Detroit Orthopaedic Clinic

Few people are more patient, tough-minded, and resourceful than the staff at the Detroit Orthopaedic Clinic, now the Detroit Institute for Children. Scores of children come under their care daily, children with varieties of handicaps, of varying degrees of severity. They deal with parents whose level of cooperation can make the therapy successful or can undo the painstaking progress. Their work is physically demanding, mentally challenging, and emotionally draining.

They analyze a child's deficiency, invent ways to re-train brain and muscles, and elicit cooperation from their little clients who don't fully understand why they have to work so hard.

The children do understand that they themselves are different. "Different" is not a positive word to a child. To a youngster, "different" means "not okay" in one way or another. He becomes shy and withdrawn or demanding and aggressive, depending on which attitude brings a satisfying response from those around him. And self-pity is always tempting.

Therapists encourage. They joke. They persist. They draw inadequate salaries and go home to their own problems. They come back to work the next day for the possibility of making a difference in the life of a handicapped child.

Larry was fitted with a padded leather helmet to protect

his head in his frequent falls. He was put through exercises at the Clinic, and his parents were to repeat these daily at home.

The speech therapist would seat him in front of a mirror, wrap her fingers with gauze, and grab his tongue, moving it for him. *P* and *B, M* and *N* sounded alike as they came from Larry's mouth, and it took a lot of practice and concentration to pronounce them to the therapist's satisfaction. It was hard for Larry to understand the need for all this, because as the sounds he made resonated inside his head, they sounded perfect to him. But the therapist gently shaped his lips, moved his tongue, coached him repetitiously. She demonstrated with her own mouth, exaggerating the motions, and as he watched her in the mirror he tried to mimic what she was doing. Often they broke into giggles at the contorted faces they made, but the therapist always went right back to work with him. There were the quiet times when she had Larry lie on the thin mat on the floor to practice relaxed breathing. He needed deep breaths to produce sustained sound for speaking.

The occupational therapist worked at developing muscle coordination from the waist up. One particular exercise involved graham cracker mush. The therapist crumbled graham crackers into a bowl and added water, stirring until the good crisp crackers became a blob of light brown mud. "Here, Larry," she said, "use this spoon and show me how well you can feed yourself."

What a waste! he thought. *I could eat crackers perfectly well with my hands, but now you've messed them up and want me to use a spoon.* He grabbed the bent plastic spoon and scooped up some of the mush. He concentrated hard to bring the spoon accurately to his mouth, but at the last split second his head jerked. The bowl of the spoon hit the corner of his mouth and twisted. Part of the mush went in, and the rest oozed down his chin toward the plastic bib.

"Pretty good. You got some that time. Let's try again." She wiped his chin and he tried again.

It wasn't always graham cracker mush. Sometimes his mom brought instant pudding. Larry preferred chocolate or strawberry because butterscotch looked too much like graham crackers.

The physical therapist made him walk, balancing himself and trying not to toe in. The braces strengthened his legs so he could go pretty fast, but as he acquired speed, he would lose balance. It took a lot of concentration, and he fell many times. But at least he never had to use crutches. He did sit-ups and climbed onto chairs and then down again, laboriously practicing under the watchful eye of the therapist.

Sue found the required weekly meetings of the mothers' group very helpful. Although she didn't realize it at the time, the D.O.C. was providing group therapy for the mothers. The staff person in charge answered their questions and gave encouragement and advice. The mothers shared resources and equipment among themselves. For instance, one of them found a shoe repair shop that sold zippers which could be laced into tennis shoes and oxfords, eliminating the need for tying shoestrings. Although tying laces and fastening buttons were life skills that were emphasized at the Clinic, there were some children who would never achieve the necessary fine-muscle coordination for these tasks. Zippers and Velcro were godsends. Mothers gladly shared information like the name of that shoe repair shop.

Most of all, there was the sheer comfort of being with others who had the same problems, the only other human beings who truly understood what it felt like to be the parent of a handicapped child.

The D.O.C. record for that first year reveals Larry's progress.

3-10-58 OT (occupational therapy) program

3-31-58 OT group, started to crawl instead of bunny-hopping—gets around in a wheeled walker

10-17-58 started a pre-dressing program

10-21-58 began to cruise around furniture

11-19-58 speech understanding good but grunts and gestures unless prodded.

Bill and Sue never forgot the lesson painfully learned from Dr. Walsh on the day of diagnosis: "Don't speak for him." In fact, following the maxim that child discipline is 90% self-discipline, they forced themselves to make Larry do as much as possible for himself. When he fell, they did not rush to pick him up. They watched to make sure he wasn't seriously hurt and then turned away, leaving him to struggle to his feet himself. It looked heartless, and it *felt* heartless to them, but helping would only weaken him. He had to learn to do everything possible for himself. They taught well-meaning relatives, and friends at church, to restrain their kind impulses. It was a tough love Larry needed.

One of his exercises involved moving his legs in a pedaling pattern. This was part of a series that led to teaching him to walk. When he had mastered the cycling movement fairly well, Bill said to Sue, "He's getting so good at that, I believe he could learn to ride a tricycle. What do you think?"

She thought of snow-covered sidewalks and the outside steps leading to their first floor apartment. And what would she do with Steve? "He probably could, but where would he ride it?"

"Here in the hallway until spring. Let's get him a trike for Christmas."

Sue readily agreed. So Santa brought Larry a shiny red tricycle a few weeks before his third birthday.

The Walls' home was festive with evergreen and ornaments and fragrant with turkey and pumpkin pies. The younger daughters, Judy and Nancy, played happily with their little nephews, Larry and Steve. Jim Wall and Bill were sprawled comfortably in front of the TV, and Mary and Sue were busy in the kitchen.

"All right, Susan, I think that's everything for now. The potatoes and green beans are on the stove, the dressing's in the oven, the cranberry relish is in the refrigerator, and the turkey is almost done. The girls can set the table, and you and I can sit down for a while."

"Okay. This is probably a good time to do Larry's exercises."

"Oh Susan! It's Christmas Day! Surely you don't have to make him do those exercises today."

Sue looked at her mother sternly. "Now, Mother. If we don't make him do them, he won't reach his full capabilities, just because we let up."

"Okay, go ahead," her mother answered meekly. "Judy, Nancy, it's time to set the table. Here, let me have the baby." So she rocked Steve while Sue put Larry through his paces.

There were many exercises, and they had changed since the last time Grandma Wall had watched. One of them involved Larry's lying on the floor on his back. Sue held a lollipop a few inches from his mouth, and he had to raise his head to get it. As he did, she moved it just out of his reach, again and again, until he had raised his head the right number of times. Then, to reward him, Sue gave him one lick of the lollipop.

"Just one lick, Susan? Surely he's earned the whole thing," Grandma urged.

"Just one lick," Sue replied, re-wrapping the lollipop. "We have to think about his teeth, too, you know."

Mary Wall had to admire her daughter and son-in-law. It was a terrible disappointment that Larry had cerebral palsy, although it was no surprise to her and Jim. They had suspected it since he was six months old. Mary had taught CP children, and she recognized the handicap when she saw it. But Susan and Bill had never mentioned that anything was wrong, so the grandparents had minded their own business as long as they could hold back. It was a great relief when they learned Larry had been to the Detroit Orthopaedic Clinic for diagnosis and treatment. And never a word of complaint or self-pity from Susan and Bill. They were just doing their very best to follow the D.O.C.'s directions. They were being so responsible that a person just had to admire them.

But that tricycle they had given the child for Christmas! Surely he'd never be able to ride it. Not that she or Jim would ever give so much as a hint that they thought he couldn't! Oh no! They had praised the gift and loved the shine in Larry's eyes when he saw it. Such a bright little fellow.

Back home again in Royal Oak after the holidays, Larry began to try the tricycle. It was something the staff at D.O.C. hadn't thought of because the sense of balance required to ride a tricycle seemed beyond Larry's capabilities at the time. But with his feet strapped to the pedals, he soon mastered the skills and tore energetically up and down the long hallway of the apartment. The understanding neighbors didn't complain about the ruckus.

D.O.C. RECORDS:
1-22-59 He can dress and undress with supervision.

Sue couldn't bear to watch him struggle to put his clothes on. There was only one way she could cope with that.

"Here are your clothes for today, Larry. You get dressed while I fix breakfast. See you in a few minutes." Then she closed the door behind her and made herself go to the kitchen. It would take him fifteen minutes or longer.

In his room, Larry tried again and again, as the pants

slipped out of his grasp and twisted out of reach. The shirt stuck over his ears, and his constantly moving hands felt for hidden armholes. Finally he emerged triumphantly to cordial praise and a hearty breakfast. Then it was time to leave for the D.O.C.

On the long drive down Woodward Avenue, there were 17 clocks—bank clocks, church clocks, storefront clocks. To the delight of the volunteer drivers from the church, Larry pointed out each one, not caring what time they told, just fascinated with clocks. To the women, it was proof that the cerebral palsy had not affected his mind. It was his way of entertaining them during the long drive.

After about a year of these thrice-weekly sessions, the D.O.C. decided Larry was ready for daily nursery school there. It was expensive, but because Bill was a veteran, the VFW provided a full scholarship. Free transportation was provided from the Detroit city limits for this day-long program. Each morning Sue drove seven or eight miles to meet the station wagon that took Larry to school. Late each afternoon, she drove again to the city limits to pick him up. Since gas cost less than 30 cents a gallon, Larry's nursery school cost the Pattons very little.

The D.O.C. record for 1959 shows how beneficial the day-long school experience was:

4-21-59 knee walking level—standing balance improving, 6 or 7 independent steps

6-3-59 short leg braces

In June, doctors recommended short leg braces to help him walk. They were expensive, and they would soon be outgrown. D.O.C. provided the first pair at no charge, used braces which had been fitted to Larry's legs. As children outgrew them, they donated their braces to D.O.C. for other children. Jim and Mary Wall paid for the second set.

With the helmet and braces, Larry was very visibly a

handicapped child. This bothered Sue's pride, but she consoled herself by thinking, *At least people can see we're doing something about it. It's not hopeless.*

D.O.C. RECORDS:

6-30-59 4 1/2 months in nursery school—toilet trained. Takes frustrations well—socially and emotionally he is 6 months ahead of his chronological age.

4

Another Kind Of Help Offered

The black and white TV flickered gray and blue into the small, crowded living room. Grandpa Patton's rugged, arthritic body was settled in his overstuffed chair too close to the television. Grandma Patton held baby Steve against her shoulder, thumping his back in time with the rhythmic creaking of her rocking chair. Bill and Sue sat on the couch. Larry wriggled restlessly between them.

"If you are sick, if you are in pain, if you have a physical problem that the doctors can't cure," intoned Oral Roberts from the video screen, "join with us as we pray in this tent. Reach out your hand and touch your TV screen, and God's healing mercies will flow into your body at home as He heals these people here. Let us pray."

"Now there's a man of God!" exclaimed Grandpa Patton, his eyes never leaving the TV. "You ever watch this, Bill?"

"No, Dad. I don't know if the Detroit stations even carry it."

"Well, you watch. You'll see people healed before your very eyes. They come forward leanin' on crutches and they walk back tall and straight, leavin' those crutches in a pile at the altar."

"Sit still, Larry," Grandma Patton said. "Sue, maybe you'd better hold him on your lap. I'm afraid those braces will snag my davenport."

Sue wrestled Larry onto her lap and held his hands, to play

pattycake. She gave Bill a side-long glance and a grim sigh. Bill's face remained impassive.

On TV, a parade of joyous, dazed, tearful people, healed of their infirmities, streamed back to their seats as the choir sang and Oral Roberts praised God.

"Tell you what, Bill," Grandpa began. "Maybe you ought to take little Larry out to one of those tent meetings. I believe in Oral Roberts' healing ministry. I just believe he could take care of Larry. What do you think?"

Bill shrugged one shoulder and said nothing, keeping his eyes stolidly on the screen. Sue squinted and unconsciously held Larry a little tighter as she waited to hear the rest of the conversation. The room was silent except for the television and the creaky rocker.

"Tell you what," Grandpa said again after a few minutes. "If you and Sue will take Larry out there, I'll pay for your trip. What do you say to that?"

Sue opened her mouth to speak, drew in her breath, and then snapped her lips shut again, looking hard at Bill. No way would she be willing to take Larry to a tent meeting and subject him and Bill and herself to all that emotional, pseudo-religious mumbo-jumbo! The offer itself infuriated her.

Without looking at his wife, Bill got the full impact of her thoughts. He felt much the same way Sue did about faith-healing, but instead of letting himself be hurt and angry at his parents' inability to accept Larry, he told himself he understood. They were much older than Sue's parents. Dad was in his eighties, and Mom was pushing seventy. They had very little formal education and had spent their whole lives in southern Indiana. Their religious beliefs were as simplistic as their entire lives were. God could mend a handicapped child and would if faith was strong. And their faith was. But Bill put his faith in the Detroit Orthopaedic Clinic.

Respect for his elders had been drummed into him along

with regular church attendance as he grew up, so he would not argue or openly disagree with them. He slid deeper into the couch, extending his feet halfway across the faded carpet, stretching his arms and curling his fists. He yawned elaborately before replying.

"Thanks, Dad. We appreciate the offer. But we feel like we're on the right track with the D.O.C. Larry's already made a lot of progress. We'll just keep on doing the exercises and see what happens."

Mr. Patton was disappointed, but he would never mention the offer again. If Bill and Sue didn't have enough faith to take Larry to Oral Roberts, it was too bad. He hated to see one of his grandsons grow up a cripple, but it was not his business. He had done all he could do.

Bill stood up, stretching again. "We'd better go. It's time to put Larry to bed. Looks like you've already taken care of Steve, Mom. Here, I'll take him."

Sue collected purse, diaper bag, and the few toys they had brought. They said perfunctory goodbyes and left.

Outside, the air seemed fresh and revitalizing. Sue drew an appreciative breath and said, "I wondered how you would handle that offer. Wasn't that something?"

"You don't mind that I turned down a free trip to Oklahoma?" Bill teased.

"Are you kidding? No way!"

The seed planted that night took several years to germinate.

5

Therapy Continues

D.O.C. RECORDS:
8-25-59 He can't rise from floor independently but is able
        to get into a chair.
10-21-59 speech plateau
1-8-60 now has play interest with brother

Family snapshots show that by this time Steve, two years
old, was almost as big as Larry. He was strong and sturdy
and had been walking for a year. A quiet, cuddly child, he
still demanded, and received, his share of attention. By the
time he was two and Larry four, their motor development
levels were similar. In fact, many people thought they were
twins. They played well together, with the usual sibling squab-
bles over toys.

D.O.C. RECORDS:
1-10-60 can feed himself using spoon

"Instead of putting hot water in the bottom of this baby
dish," suggested the occupational therapist, "let's try weighted
BB's. Then the dish will stay put when Larry pushes his spoon
against the walls to get a bite."
The caseworker advised, "Take Larry with you and go out
to eat whenever you can. He needs to learn he has a right

to be in public places as much as anyone else. It will give him confidence and keep him from being self-conscious."

So Larry went to carry-in dinners at church, to picnics, and, when his parents could afford it, to restaurants. At church everyone was glad to see his progress, but in restaurants, people stared at the family with the two little boys, one in helmet and braces. Larry fed himself, usually finger food. Bill ate, oblivious, and Sue helped Steve and tried not to notice the stares. It was a big step toward self-sufficiency for Larry to feed himself. She was proud of him, but the curious stares bothered her. She wanted to turn to the other diners and say, "He has cerebral palsy. Now eat your dinners."

So much progress had been made that school year that the entry in the D.O.C. record for 5-24-60 reads, "Request placement in Tyler Orthopedic Unit." The staff at D.O.C. thought that at age four and one half, Larry was ready for public school! What a milestone!

For the summer of 1960, Bill had a job as summer recreation director at Wing Lake School in Bloomfield Hills, one of the northern suburbs. When a neighbor offered the use of her pool to add swimming to the program, Bill had been able to get Sue a job as lifeguard in the mornings. But Larry had to be at the D.O.C. in downtown Detroit for nursery school every day.

Early each morning, Bill and Sue buckled Larry and Steve into the two car seats in the back of the Dodge and drove south into the city to deliver Larry to nursery school. Then they headed north for the suburb where the recreation program was held. They worked through the morning, with Steve, then three years old, participating with the youngest children.

At noon, Sue slipped shorts and a blouse on over her swim suit, grabbed sandwiches and lemonade, settled Steve in his car-seat with his lunch, and ate her lunch in the front seat as she drove back into Detroit to pick up Larry. His lunch was provided there.

From there they drove home and rested for about an hour and then back in the car to drive out to Bloomfield Hills to pick up Bill when the afternoon session of recreation ended. Steve must have felt he grew up in that car seat.

They were also involved in evening activities. Bill played on the church softball team. The whole family went to watch these games. Bill and Sue were in a couples' group at church, and Sue was circle chairman that year. They played cards regularly, too, so they did the normal things that young families do, besides all the exercises and the frantic scheduling to meet Larry's needs.

This was good in many ways. They certainly had no time to feel sorry for themselves. Neither was there time to ask the utterly unanswerable questions about Larry's future. They tried to have a positive attitude, to believe in Larry and themselves. They believed that with God's help they would at least survive and maybe even succeed.

In September, 1960, Larry went to the Orthopedic Unit at Tyler School, part of the Oakland County Intermediate School District's special education program. It cost nothing; even transportation was provided by the school district. A taxi picked Larry up every morning at the apartment and returned him that afternoon.

There he met his friend Larry Kuehn, one of three or four classmates who had spina bifida; Joe Stack and Danny and Marc Kramer, children with muscular dystrophy; and several others with cerebral palsy, including Larry's friend, Kevin Degan. Larry Patton seemed to be the most mobile member of the class.

Five teachers presided over the Tyler Orthopedic Unit: Betty Farah, the physical therapist; Terry Harding, the occupational therapist; Dorothy Peters, the speech therapist; Marsha Snider, the academic teacher; and Shirley Thompson, the pre-school teacher. In addition, there were two aides, Marian Dawson and Audrey Chute.

By second grade, Larry was going into regular classes for English and math, coming back to the orthopedic unit for the rest of the day. There he had his own little "office," a study carrel where he did assignments and kept his papers. After the initial fear and shyness, he loved going into the regular classrooms. He felt important and superior as he left the orthopedic unit and business-like when he returned with work to do. Some of his orthopedic friends never left the room for other classes.

At recess, the orthopedic group loved playing tee-ball. With the help of the therapists, they swung the bat at a ball balanced on a 24-inch tee. One day Larry Kuehn, strapped into his wheelchair, hit a triple. Wildly, Larry Patton pushed his friend around the bases and in the excitement tipped him over.

What a commotion! Larry Kuehn screamed, frightened though not really hurt. The therapists came flying to the rescue. Larry Patton was terrified. "I didn't mean to tip him over!" he insisted again and again, tears streaming down his dusty, flushed face. In his agitation, his speech became incoherent and his arms waved wildly. "I didn't mean to tip him over!"

Betty righted the wheelchair and calmed Larry Kuehn. Terri soothed Larry Patton. "Deep breaths, Larry. Calm down, now. Of course you didn't mean to tip him over. We all know you wouldn't do that. Look, he's all right. See?"

Larry Kuehn managed a plucky grin through his tears. Larry Patton, greatly relieved, began to draw some deep breaths, trying to relax. Great shudders and sniffles lasted for another half hour. The game resumed, but for the best interest of everyone, Larry was not allowed to push wheelchairs around bases again.

Following directions from the doctors at the D.O.C., the

three therapists at Tyler put Larry through prescribed treatment. He knew they were important, necessary, yet how he resisted doing the exercises and tasks! He didn't have time! He had to get his lessons done to cut down on homework. Mom was strict about his after-school routine: change clothes (What a waste! It took forever!), snack, and do homework before you go out to play. By the time Larry started his homework, Steve had whizzed through and was already outside shooting baskets at the goal Dad had put up in the driveway. While Larry laboriously guided the fat pencil around the correct answers on a worksheet, he could hear the shouts of the neighborhood kids as they dribbled, passed, and shot the ball.

But Mom and the therapists were firm, no matter what short-cut Larry invented. In P. T., Betty led him through leg lifts, one after another. As his muscles strengthened, she added sandbags over his legs. Rewards helped. One time when his cooperation was particularly poor, she said, "See that ladder over there, Larry? If you really work on these leg lifts, I'll let you climb the ladder when you're done."

The ladder stretched from floor to ceiling, an absolutely forbidden and consequently mocking challenge. For two years he had eyed that ladder, longing to pull himself up those rungs of pipe firmly fastened to the wall. All the children had been threatened with their lives if they climbed it without supervision, so he never had. Now Betty was offering him the chance.

With sparkling eyes glued to the ladder, he performed the leg lifts with concentrated vigor. Finally Betty was satisfied. He ran to the ladder, wrapped both hands around a high rung, and planted his right foot on the bottom rung. He pulled himself up till his left foot found its place beside the right one. Holding tight with his left hand and pressing his body tightly against the ladder, he stretched his right arm up till his grasping fingers found the next rung. Right foot up. Left hand up. Left foot up.

Betty's voice coaching him sounded farther away as he climbed. "Now you've gone high enough. How are you going to get back down? Think about it."

Larry clutched the ladder and thought. His hands were beginning to sweat and the rung felt slippery. He wiped his right palm on the seat of his pants quickly and then grabbed the rung just below the one his left hand seemed riveted to. Gingerly he lowered his body and felt with his right foot for the next rung down. There! It worked. Left hand wiped on seat of pants then next to right hand. Left foot next to right foot. Right hand down one rung. Right foot down again.

"Good job, Larry!" Betty cheered. "Just two more steps to go and you're down."

His arches ached from balancing on the rungs. His arms quivered from the exertion. His legs trembled from the leg lifts and the climb. But when Larry found himself firmly on the floor again, he squeaked triumphantly, "That was really neat!"

Occupational therapy was more fun than physical therapy because he got to keep what he made: a jigsaw puzzle pedaled out on the theracycle, woven potholders for Mom and Grandma Wall for Christmas gifts, a board with jar lids nailed on so Dad could store nails, screws, and bolts conveniently. But Terri was as much a slave driver as Betty. Larry asked to take the board with jar lids home to sand it. He worked hours on it, scouring it with sand paper wrapped around a wooden block. The board was finally smooth and clean, and Larry proudly carried it back to school.

"See what a good job I did?" He displayed his work to Terri.

"*What* good job? What's this?" She pointed to an ugly smudge on the back.

"Oh no! That must have happened on the bus. It's all dirty!"

"The only way to get dirt off a board is to sand it! Get busy, Larry!"

What a waste! All that work at home, and now I have to do it all over again. Silently, doggedly, he scrubbed the board until it passed Terri's inspection. She rumpled his hair and said, "Well, Larry, you've really sanded that board. It's getting kinda thin, but it looks great!"

Every six months, Larry had to go back to the D.O.C. for a check-up. In their evaluative conference, the doctors eliminated some exercises and added others. Always, Bill and Sue did exactly what was recommended, no more and certainly no less. These doctors were the experts. They knew their business. The Pattons pinned their hopes for Larry on following their instructions to the letter and praying every day that God would help Larry reach his full potential.

6

The Tyler Parents Orthopedic Group

"We *can't* let them keep us from having a summer program! It's too hard on our kids!" Rosalie Kramer exclaimed when she heard that there would be no funds for special education during the summer vacation of 1961. She faced the other parents whose handicapped children were classmates of her two sons in the Tyler Orthopedic Unit. The young couples had met every month during the past school year, at the request of the teachers, to learn together how to cope with being parents of handicapped children. It was a discouraged, listless group tonight at the February meeting.

"I know you're right," admitted Don Degan. "Kevin couldn't keep up with the neighborhood kids last summer and really felt left out." Kevin's cerebral palsy is somewhat more involved than Larry's.

"Why, last summer Marc spent many an afternoon tied to a tree. He wanted to play with the other children so much that he was always willing to be the bad guy in a game of Cops and Robbers. Many times I'd find him still tied there, long after the others had gone off to play softball or some other game. In their haste to get on with play, they'd forget he was tied. And Marc can't undo the ropes himself," Rosalie explained. Both Marc and his brother Danny had muscular dystrophy.

"It's not only the socialization," added Betty Farah, the

physical therapist for the unit. "After a summer of idleness, it takes us two months to bring the children back up to the physical capability level they had last spring."

Frank Gallagher said, "Well, I don't know where else to turn. We've petitioned the Cerebral Palsy Association, Crippled Children's Association, the Shriners, local, county, and state boards of education, and all the recreation departments in the area. If there's no money, there's no money!"

The very excellence of the program at the Tyler Orthopedic Unit made the abrupt break-off for summer vacation a dismal change for the children. None of the parents wanted another summer of seeing their children apathetically backsliding.

Larry had never experienced the summer let-down that the parents were talking about because he had gone to the summer program at D.O.C. But as Bill and Sue listened, they knew they didn't want him to lose much of the gains he was making at Tyler.

The group was silent. Defeat seemed inevitable.

Then Rosalie asked, "Has anyone ever considered raising the money ourselves?"

The words hung in mid-air. Then ideas and energy began to flood the room.

"How would we begin?"

"How much would we need?"

"How about giving a card party?"

"Could we have it here at school?"

"Where would we get the prizes?"

". . . the refreshments?"

"Where do we get tables and chairs?"

"If we're going to get into fund-raising, we need to incorporate and get ourselves recognized as a tax-exempt charity, don't we?"

So they named themselves the Tyler Parents Orthopedic Group and began forming concrete plans.

Rosalie Kramer was named benefit chairman. She had started the whole thing, after all! They agreed that the party would have to be clear profit, so the parents volunteered to donate everything—from cream and sugar to the prizes.

"I don't care where you get the prizes, from your basements or from local merchants, or whether you sew an apron or make potholders. But if this is to be a success, each one of us has to do his part," Rosalie exhorted them.

The Berkley Board of Education gave permission for the party to be held at Tyler School. And the parents outdid themselves, donating 80 prizes and selling over 300 tickets. Five hundred dollars was realized from the card party.

But that was far short of the $1840 needed to run the summer program, from 8:30 A.M. to 12:30 P.M. five days a week for six weeks at Tyler.

Undaunted, Rosalie went over to the school and took movies of the children at work and play. Then she and Sue and Carol Degan, along with the two teachers, became a sort of Speakers' Bureau. They went out to tell the story and show the film to any club or organization that would listen.

The Berkley PTA Council contributed $800 to the summer program, and many other cash donations came in. But much more than money accrued.

Organizations and individuals became interested in the children and volunteered their help. Several Junior League members agreed to serve as chauffeurs, eliminating the need for expensive taxi service to transport the children to and from school. One sorority offered to purchase some braces and other equipment the children needed. Eight young teenagers asked if they could help as teacher aides.

The summer program was a great success. It was a day-camp atmosphere, with a constant flow of activities, songs, and games. The emphasis was not academic—the school year was long enough for that—but social and physical. The daily schedule alternated from indoor, fine-motor skill activities; to rhythm games and songs accompanied by motions; to outdoor, gross-motor activities such as T-ball and relay races. The children not only maintained their end-of-school levels of achievement but also enjoyed an active, sociable summer, not having to feel left out by more "normal" children in their neighborhoods.

And a special thing happened to the parents, too. They became a close group. They had only one common factor—being parents of handicapped children. It is unlikely that they would have formed any kind of bond otherwise, because their economic status, race, neighborhoods, religious affiliations, educations, vocations, and recreational interests were different. But as a result of their membership in the Tyler Parents Orthopedic Group, they formed lasting friendships, and they gained understanding in the areas where they differed.

The summer program of 1961 was so successful that the group continued the project through the next several years. Sue was elected treasurer for three years, and then, in 1965, she became president.

"The October meeting of the Tyler Parents Orthopedic Group will come to order." Sue nervously checked her agenda. It was only her second time to preside, and this was the most important meeting of the year. Of course Don Degan, past president, was right there to help out, and Rosalie Kramer and Jean Kuehn were ready with their presentations. "Could we hear the minutes of the September meeting, please?"

The secretary stood to read from her ledger: "The September meeting of the TPOG was called to order by President Mrs. William Patton with about 40 members present. Minutes were read and approved, and a balance in the treasury of $458 was reported by the treasurer, Don Degan. A letter from Harold B. Grayson, Director of the Berkley School District Special Education Program, was read. He reported that 30 children participated in the summer program, along with the physical therapist, the speech therapist, the recreational director and her aide, and teenage volunteers. Mrs. Marsha Snider, academic teacher of the Tyler Orthopedic Unit, commented on how well the children have started school this year. Their regression because of summer vacation has been minimal because of participation in the summer program.

"Mrs. Fred Kuehn, co-chairman of the Open House Committee, presented plans for that event, to be completed at the October meeting. The business part of the meeting was adjourned, and Mrs. Betty Farah, physical therapist, introduced Dr. John Smithson, a local dentist, who gave a talk on dental care for children with handicaps. A question and answer period followed his presentation, and then refreshments were served. Respectfully submitted, Mrs. John Belknap, secretary."

"Any additions or corrections? Then the minutes will stand approved as read. Thank you, Kathy. Treasurer's report, please?"

"Same balance as last month, but there'll be plenty of bills to pay for this Open House before our next meeting, I'm sure."

Everyone agreed with that prediction. This Open House to thank the benefactors who had made the summer program possible was one of their biggest ventures ever. They had invited local members of the Michigan State Legislature, hoping to convince them to sponsor funding legislation. The possibilities of generating future support were tantalizing, but the reverse was ominous. What if they overlooked someone? What if it didn't come off as a first class event? How much could that hurt their future effectiveness?

"Okay, let's hear how plans are coming along for the Open House. Who's to report first, Jean or Rosalie?" Sue asked. "Remember we decided to devote this whole meeting to getting ready for the Open House on October 27. We don't have anything else planned for this evening, so let's get to work. Jean?"

The parents were seated on folding chairs around the low tables of the orthopedic classroom. Behind them, parallel bars, work benches, a weaving loom, and other special equipment filled the edges and corners of the cheerful room. The walls were covered with charts of children's progress, decorations of fall leaves, and student art work.

Jean Kuehn leaned forward, spreading open a folder with notes on all sizes of paper. She held up a three-by-five printed card and said, "These invitations have gone out to over 30 organizations that have contributed to our summer program, to merchants who have donated prizes for our annual card parties, and to elected officials like our state senators and representatives, Governor Romney, and our members of Congress."

"Did you forget LBJ?" someone asked.

Recognizing the teasing tone, Jean nevertheless replied quite seriously, "We invited people who might vote for legislation to help us."

"Well, he *signs* legislation, doesn't he? And remember, he's a millionaire himself."

"I'll invite him tomorrow!" Jean grinned. "It says on the invitation that there will be entertainment by the Sweet Adelines," she went on. "Bless their hearts, it's not enough for them to help finance our summer program—they want to provide entertainment at our thank-you party!"

"Hey, that'll be great!"

"Have you invited the press and the radio and TV people?"

"Yes, we've sent invitations to all of them in the area, and you'll be seeing publicity about the Open House everywhere in the next two weeks. Flowers have been ordered to decorate the refreshment table, and corsages for our officers, the teachers, and the therapists."

"Speaking of refreshments, we're counting on each one of you to bring cookies or finger sandwiches. Over 200 RSVP's have already come in, and we sure don't want to run out of food! Now, Rosalie, tell 'em about the program."

"Okay, when the guests come in, the first thing they'll see will be large, individual photos of each child. Frank Gallagher, our resident photographer . . ." She nodded in his direction as the group smiled in appreciation. "Frank has taken these pictures here at school and enlarged them. This row of 30 photos will be like a receiving line as the people enter. The therapists will lead tours of the unit and explain the uses of equipment in the three therapy rooms. The pre-school and academic classrooms will also be open for inspection. The regular classroom next door will be used to show the film of this year's summer program, made by Frank Gallagher . . ."

Frank rose gallantly and added, "And narrated by Rosalie Kramer."

She smiled modestly and continued. "In the pre-school and academic rooms there will be the refreshment table and another table to display handcrafted articles created by the students. And the Sweet Adelines will perform in the gym. Sue, will you greet people at the door, or make a welcoming speech, or what?"

"Both. I'll be at the door as they come in, and then when most of them have moved to the gym, I'll make a little speech welcoming them and thanking them. I'll introduce the legislators then. Next, I'll tell them our Speakers' Bureau will be glad to bring the film and a speaker to one of their meetings this year, just check with Jean Kuehn or me. And I guess that's the time to read this letter I received from Governor Romney."

Simultaneous responses were heard:

"Wow, a letter from the governor!"

"Oh, he's not coming! Too bad!"

"He'll be touring the Far East, probably watching the Japanese make cars, but he sent this letter." She skimmed it rapidly. "He sums up what we've accomplished so far and concludes,

> 'It is my strong feeling that an organization such as the Tyler Parents' Orthopedic Group serves a wholly necessary purpose in our society which is groping forward toward answers which are not yet fully known. I commend the members of your organization and wish you the maximum of success in your efforts during the coming year.'"

"Yeah, be sure to read that! It should impress the state legislators, if they come."

Jean Kuehn said, "So far we've had acceptances from State Representatives Albert Kramer and Daniel Cooper, State Senator Sander Levin, and from Congressman William Broomfield. We should be able to introduce the program to them, and hopefully the State Legislature will help fund the program in the future."

"Great!"

"What a party!"

Jean concluded the report, "Yes, I think it will be quite a party. Remember we're counting on all of you to bring refreshments, and please plan to stay after to clean up. These rooms have to be ready for classes as usual the next day. Any other questions or comments?"

Marsha Snider, the academic teacher of the orthopedic unit, stood to speak. Everyone became quiet.

"It's a great idea to have a party to thank all those people who have helped, and I'm sure it will be a lovely evening. You've thought of everything. But speaking for the therapists and myself, I'd like to thank *you*! This parents' group is really special. There's a closeness and a spirit of cooperation here that we've never seen before in a parents' group. Usually we sponsor these groups to help the parents cope with their children's handicaps. But you've gone far beyond that. Not only are you coping very well individually, but with your joint efforts you've given your children more than we've ever been able to offer them. And seeing you working so hard has inspired us to be better teachers and therapists. So I think it's time someone said a big thank-you to each one of you!"

Betty Farah, one of the therapists, began the applause as Marsha sat down, and then the parents joined in, applauding themselves as tears streamed down their cheeks. It was a special moment when they paused to acknowledge what they had accomplished, but it was characteristically brief. There was always too much work to do to wallow in emotion, whether congratulatory or self-pitying.

"No further business?" Sue asked, through a rainbow of happy tears. "Meeting adjourned. See you all on the 27th!"

The thank-you reception was a great success. The parents could tell as the evening went along by the interested questions people asked and the comments about the special equipment.

"What is this theracycle?"

"It works like an exercise bike. By pedaling, the child strengthens leg muscles so he can walk better. And the pedaling also powers this jig-saw so he can cut pieces for various craft projects in occupational therapy."

"But isn't this room physical therapy?"

"Yes," Betty smiled, "but we overlap all the time. Basically, physical therapy is for gross motor development, and occupational therapy is for fine motor skills. But we train the whole child, all the time. You'll see what I mean when you visit the occupational therapy and speech therapy rooms."

"Good idea!"

In the occupational therapy room were some standing work tables that Bill and another dad had built, as well as the ordinary low tables found in regular grade-school classrooms.

"What are these for?" asked a visitor.

"These enable the children to stand up while they work with their hands. It strengthens their leg muscles and improves balance."

"Great!"

And in the speech therapy room there were mirrors and talking boards to be explained.

"Here a child can see what his facial muscles are doing when he tries to pronounce a word. He watches the therapist and tries to imitate the way she moves her lips and tongue to get a particular sound."

"Look at all these flash cards stuck everywhere!" a guest exclaimed.

"Yes, these are words they need in their academic classrooms. We especially work on pronouncing words they use in classes."

"What are these charts of words with pictures?"

"Those are the talking boards. A child whose speech is so severely handicapped that his sounds are unintelligible can point to words or ideas he wants to express."

"Amazing!"

At the end of the evening, the members of the Michigan State Legislature came to Sue.

Senator Levin said, "It's just tremendous what you've done here and with your summer program. But you shouldn't have to work so hard. You have more than enough to do, just being parents of handicapped children."

Representative Kramer added, "We've decided to co-sponsor a bill for the State to fund 75% of the cost of summer special education programs. People all over the state need what you have, and we should have been providing it all along."

Sue was elated. "Oh, that's wonderful! What can we do

to help?"

"Give us a resume of the TPOG's history, including any legislative petitions," replied Representative Cooper, "and if some of you could come up to Lansing to speak at the hearings on the bill, that would be fine. We'll keep in touch."

The bill was passed, and since 1966, handicapped children all over Michigan have benefitted from the tireless efforts of the Tyler Parents Orthopedic Group.

7

Tears In The Night

Slow tears seeped from Sue's wide-open eyes, ran sideways over the bridge of her nose, and dropped silently onto her pillow. Street light through the venetian blinds made diagonal prison bars across their small bedroom. Beside her, Bill snored softly. Upstairs, Larry and Steve were curled in cocoons of dreams.

She sniffled quietly, afraid of disturbing Bill but hoping he would waken and comfort her. At least talk to her. At the very least, listen to her!

He slept on.

A car crunched past on the snow-covered street, then silence. Sue sat up, dragging the covers with her. Bill pulled them back around his shoulders, turned in his sleep, swallowed noisily, and then breathed peacefully through his nose.

She gasped as her feet struck the cold floor boards. Ignoring the fuzzy slippers and her long quilted robe, she padded barefooted to the kitchen and flipped on the light. She filled the tea kettle, clamped the whistling cap on, banged it onto a burner of the stove, and wrenched the knob to high.

Bill slept through the light and sounds.

Sue paced the circular pattern of the front half of their Cape Cod-style cottage, from the kitchen, through the dinette with the curtained bay windows, past the front door, turning left into the cozy living room cluttered with papers and school books, toward the tiny hallway with six door frames, one from the living room, next one to the bathroom, then adjacent doorways to guest room and their bedroom, the door to the stairway leading to the boys' big play-and bedroom under the eaves, and the doorway back into the kitchen.

The second time through the dark living room, she stubbed her toe on the coffee table. "Ouch!" she exclaimed aloud and then collapsed into Bill's big chair, drew up her knees and massaged the injured toe. She gave in to audible sobs.

How can he sleep when I'm so miserable? How can he just drop off to sleep as if we hadn't a care in the world? He doesn't care!

We eat out and people stare at Larry, and Bill doesn't even notice! Larry and Steve get into fights, and I'm so scared Larry will bang his head and get even more handicapped, and Bill says, "Let 'em alone! They're just acting normal."

Normal! Nobody's normal around here! Larry may never be able to live alone, Steve is getting short-changed of attention because of Larry, we don't have enough money to live like normal people, and Bill has no ambition! He just doesn't care!

She stomped into the bathroom for a tissue and prolonged the nose-blowing for Bill's benefit. He didn't stir.

Back to the kitchen, where the tea kettle was beginning to hum gently. Past the built-in china cabinet, through the dinette, across the cold tiles of the front hall, back into the living room. This time she turned on the small lamp on the antique blanket chest. The trajectory of the light hit the mirror over the couch and cast a distant beam on Bill's peaceful face in their bedroom.

At church Sally says Phil is climbing the corporate ladder with G.M. At Bloomfield Hills, Wes is working on his administrator's license so he can get to be a principal and then some day a superintendent. That's where the money is—in administration! And what is Bill getting his master's degree in? Counseling and guidance! Those people are on the same salary schedule with classroom teachers! There's no future there. No matter what I say, and Lord knows I've said plenty, he keeps on signing up for counseling and guidance. And you watch! Even after he gets his master's, he'll probably never even move up to a high school as counselor. He'll spend the rest of his life in elementary P.E. in Bloomfield Hills, making a piddly income in one of the wealthiest suburbs in the nation!

The whistling tea kettle let out a screech. Sue raced to the kitchen, grabbed the hot handle without a potholder, and slammed it onto a cold burner. She listened as she blew on her blistered fingers. No sound from the boys' room, thank goodness. And of course no rise from Bill!

God, it's just not fair, she complained. *Not cerebral palsy and being poor, too. I could handle either one by itself, but don't You think both is a bit much?*

She picked up the tea kettle with the potholder of colorful woven jersey loops that Larry had made in occupational therapy for her Christmas present and poured the steaming water over instant coffee in her favorite mug, a gift from Steve. She stirred the coffee and clanged the spoon onto the ceramic spoon holder on the stove, then crossed to the round dinette table, dragged a chair away, and sat down heavily. The society page of yesterday's paper lay on the place mats Larry had made as another O.T. project.

"Dance to Benefit Crippled Children," the headline announced, and the accompanying picture showed some of Detroit's wealthiest socialites dressed in glittering evening clothes.

Everybody does so much for handicapped children, and it's truly wonderful. But I wish, just once, they'd do something for the parents. Send us flowers, or invite us to one of these balls. Suddenly she felt like Cinderella huddled in the ashes. *Of course if I went, someone would have to give me a gown to wear!* she thought bitterly. *It's not fair! And Bill just doesn't care!*

Her anger flared again. She pushed aside the mug of coffee, scraped back the chair, flung open the front door, and threw herself on the front steps. The door swung shut behind her with a significant click.

The icy night air hit her as forcefully as a bucket of water thrown in the face of hysteria. She jerked her head and stared blankly at the empty street. She sucked in her frosty breath, and her throat, swollen from crying, constricted painfully.

You can't run away—you have nowhere to go! a silent voice mocked her.

That's right, she thought slowly, laboriously. *I can't. I don't.*

She turned to face the familiar door and tried the knob. She was locked out!

Her flannel nightgown seemed thin as voile. Her bare feet ached and then turned numb. Shivering uncontrollably, she rang the doorbell with one hand and pounded the door knocker with the other. "Bill! Let me in!"

After a few minutes the porch light flashed on and the door opened wide. There was Bill, in his rumpled striped pajamas and spiky hair, staring at her and saying, "What on earth are you doing out there?"

She leaped into the comforting warmth and slammed the door against the cold empty night. Her teeth chattered so hard she couldn't answer.

Bill led her, shivering, to the living room. She huddled on the couch, her cold feet tucked under her. He wrapped the knitted pink afghan around her. "What were you doing out there?" he repeated.

"Coffee," she stuttered. "The mug on the table."

He brought it and stood looking down at her, waiting.

She wrapped her cold fingers around the still-steaming mug and inhaled the warmth. The shudders subsided.

"Well?"

"I was just upset," she began sheepishly.

"About what?"

"Oh, about Larry, and money." She was deliberately vague.

"What about 'em?"

"I just got upset. And you kept right on sleeping! Don't things ever bother you?"

"Sure," he answered calmly, "but there's no sense losin' sleep over 'em. C'mon back to bed."

Why not? she thought, thawing from the hot coffee and the wooly afghan, suddenly sleepy. Bill turned out the lights, and she followed him obediently to bed.

Why can't I ever tell him what I'm really thinking? she wondered drowsily. She rolled over under the blankets and studied the outline of Bill's head, shoulder, elbow, hip, and leg. He looked like the skyline of the southern Indiana hills. Timeless. Solid. Unchanging. Not someone to confide in, but somehow reassuring. She snuggled up against his back and drifted off to sleep.

8

Parents Grow, Too

"The parents of handicapped children often benefit from professional counseling," the psychology instructor told the graduate class. Bill put down his pencil to listen carefully. "Mothers especially are simply so busy with day-to-day care and dealing with crises as they arise that they don't have time to deal with their own emotions. Many times they are repressing feelings: Guilt: 'What have I done to deserve a handicapped child?' Fear: 'Will he live? Will he be a burden to us in our old age or to his brothers and sisters when we're gone?' Resentment: 'This child takes all my time and attention! What about *my* life?' Professional counseling can be very beneficial in cases like this."

Bill grabbed his pencil and wrote quickly. The truth of the professor's words hit him with awful clarity. Their lives had been hectically overscheduled ever since Larry had been enrolled at the D.O.C.

With Larry now attending the orthopedic unit at Tyler, Sue had more free time than ever before, although she was teaching adult education classes two nights a week to finance Bill's master's degree.

But even with the additional time at home during the days, she couldn't seem to settle down and take care of the house and cook, as Bill wished she would. Instead, she restlessly filled her days with church work and P.T.A., especially the

Tyler Parents Orthopedic Group. He knew that her activities were worthwhile and important, but she seemed so . . . well, she certainly didn't seem happy. She was always harping at him about something or other. Nag, nag, nag! And the other week when she locked herself out in the middle of the night! He wondered how often she got up in the night to pace around and cry. Maybe repressed feelings were catching up with her.

If I suggest she go for counseling, she'll accuse me of thinking she's crazy. But if I suggest the minister, instead of a psychiatrist, maybe she'll go. Bill had it all figured out.

"How was your class this evening?" Sue asked as Bill dropped his books with a thud on the table.

"Okay. Got a cup of coffee and a piece of pie?"

"Instant coffee's on the stove, but you *know* there's no pie. If you want pie, you'll have to go down to The Nugget to get some. I certainly haven't had time to bake a pie! Whatever made you ask for pie, Bill?"

"I *want* some. I'm hungry." He fixed himself a cup of coffee and sat down at the table where she was grading papers. He opened his notebook and read aloud to her. "'The parents of handicapped children often benefit from professional counseling. Mothers especially repress their feelings because they're just too busy to deal with them.' That's what the teacher said tonight. How does that hit you?"

"You think I'm repressing my feelings? You think I need counseling? You think I'm crazy or something?"

"Hold on," he said quietly. "He said you *may benefit*."

"*Me*? You talked about me in your class tonight?"

"No, no! Calm down. He said professional counseling may benefit parents of handicapped children, to help them get their feelings out and deal with them. And I thought of you. You sure have been busy ever since Larry was diagnosed, and you *may* have some repressed feelings about his CP that ought to be explored. That doesn't mean I think you're crazy. I thought maybe you might talk to Reverend Kirkman at church and see if he could help you identify any of these feelings and work through them. What do you think?"

"I don't know. I don't think I need counseling. And if I asked Tom Kirkman for an appointment like that, what would he think?"

"He gets requests like that all the time. He's mentioned that he does a lot of counseling," he reminded her.

"Yeah," she said doubtfully. "Well, I'll think about it. You know a piece of pie *would* taste good. Why don't you run down to The Nugget and bring home some for me, too. Get a whole pie, and I'll put some in your lunch tomorrow."

"I do not think it was God's will for Larry to have cerebral palsy," Tom Kirkman stated quietly.

"You don't?" Sue stared in disbelief. "I've always accepted the CP on the basis that it was God's plan and therefore it must be right, for Larry and for us."

"No. I believe God wants all His children to be healthy and whole, sound of limb and mind. He is a loving God, after all."

"Then what went wrong? I mean, I know what went wrong, but if God doesn't want Larry to have CP, why did He let it happen?" Sue's glasses slipped down, but she was too agitated to push them back up. The whole foundation of her acceptance of Larry's condition was under question.

"Sue, I think there is a difference between God's *perfect* will and His *permissive* will. His perfect will is for Larry to be fine. But the accident at birth happened because of His natural laws. If He over-rode those natural laws every time a human being was in trouble, we couldn't count on any consistency in nature. Instead, He permits these things to happen, He suffers with us, and through His love and saving grace, He works with us to make good come from even the worst tragedies. That's what Paul is talking about in Romans 8:28: 'And we know that all things work together for good to them that love God, to them who are called according to His purpose.'"

"Well, I can't see that any good has come from it. I'll have to think about that!"

"Okay. Do you want an appointment for next week? Check with the secretary, and she'll put you on the schedule."

Sue nodded, mumbled goodbye, and left the office without speaking to the secretary. She hurried blindly down the long hall, her footsteps echoing in her ears.

She pulled open the heavy, silent door of the lounge. The coolness and muted colors drew her in, and she sank into a cushioned couch. For several minutes her anguished sobs rang out.

God, if it isn't Your will, why did You let it happen? You're supposed to be in charge of our lives. How could You let such an awful thing happen? All this time I thought it was Your plan, and I had to accept it. Now Tom says, no, it was just an accident that You let happen!

Her shoulders heaved. Her breath came in wrenching gasps. Self-consciously she was half afraid someone would hear her, and yet she half hoped someone would come in to comfort her.

No one came.

What possible good could come from this? Larry's crippled! He can hardly talk. He can hardly dress and feed himself. Strangers stare. Do-gooders give him too much attention. Steve feels left out. What good could possibly come from that?

Her eyes stung and her vision was blurred. Her sides hurt from the force of her crying. Her head throbbed as the tears subsided, and her heart, an icy stone, weighted the top of her knotted stomach. The room was silent. If God had heard, He had not chosen to defend Himself.

The burden of doubt that Dr. Kirkman had given her grew heavier with passing weeks. It became harder for her to watch Larry do even his most accomplished tasks. If she had nagged Bill before, now she became an absolute shrew.

Her mother, visiting for a weekend, even warned her, "Susan, Bill's going to lose all his self-confidence if you don't quit picking at him like that."

Sue honestly couldn't understand what her mother was talking about.

It was about that time she noticed her vision was blurred. She was in church, singing, when she shut her right eye. The words in the hymn book ran together. The next morning she obtained the name of a reputable ophthamologist from the church secretary.

Dr. Fox told her, "You have an infection in the chorioid part of your eye, and it has hemorrhaged. The infection is not primarily located in your eye, however. It's somewhere else in your body. Here's a prescription for cortisone to clear your eye, but I want you to have a complete physical. We must locate the source of this infection."

The clock read three A.M. Upstairs the window fan whirred softly, drawing cool air through the house still warm from the July day. Bill and the boys slept. Sue paced in the dark and cried.

What if I go blind? What would I do? What would Larry do? Even though she knew exactly where every piece of furniture was in the living room, in the dark they looked much larger and ill-defined. The street light shone in, casting shadows that should have been familiar after so many sleepless nights, but her blurred eyes couldn't distinguish shadows from real objects. She walked slowly, feeling her way around.

At any time, of course, she could have turned on a light,

but she took perverse pleasure in punishing herself, feeding
the terror that grew in her mind.

*Oh God! I get it! You're making me go blind so I won't
have to see Larry anymore. It's all because I'm not satisfied
with his condition. I want him to walk straight so no one will
know there's anything wrong with him. You're going to take
away my vision so I can't see him stumble around or watch
people stare!*

*No! Please, God, no! I know appearances aren't that im-
portant! Really, God! I'm satisfied! He has made a lot of progress, I realize that! I'll not let people staring bother me so
much anymore. Please, God, heal my eyes!*

She fell onto the couch and cried herself to sleep.

The blurred vision in her eye cleared up, but the infection
persisted. Her family doctor examined her but couldn't find
the source. Finally she went to an allergist who found that
she was allergic to her own bacteria. He ordered a serum
which was injected into her bloodstream weekly for over a
year until she tested all right. Her eyes are well now except
for a tiny scar.

In the fall of 1964, Kathie Irwin invited Sue to attend a newly
organized women's prayer group. Sue really wasn't interested,
but she valued Kathie's friendship. Kathie had already invited
the Pattons to go to Family Camp, and they had not gone.
She had invited Sue to do some other things in the church
that Sue had not been able to do. So Sue agreed to go to the
prayer group, primarily because she didn't want to offend
Kathie by saying no again.

She was so skeptical about it that she hesitated to tell Bill
she was going. She was sure he would think she was becoming

some sort of religious kook, joining a prayer group. To her amazement, Bill thought it was a good idea and encouraged her to go. It sounded like the weekly prayer meetings he had known as a child, and he thought it would "do her good."

It took only one meeting with this small group of Christian friends for Sue to realize it was worth the effort. They were concerned about the problems of daily living. Here she found support, love, a place where she could confide her worries about Larry. Most of all, she found people who had a real relationship with Jesus Christ, something she did not have.

At that point, Sue and Bill were very active in the church. They believed in God, they had accepted Christ as their Savior, and they prayed (but not together) for forgiveness of their sins. But they did not know Jesus as Lord of their lives.

The women in this group were of various ages and at various stages of Christian growth. A couple of them, Eunice Bitzer and Dorothy Harrison, had probably grown more, spiritually, at that point than the rest of them. All of them were open and loving. Sue had a lot of insecure feelings and many questions, but no matter what she did or what kind of questions she raised, they still loved her.

As she met with her prayer group over a period of months, she became aware of a quality of life, a relationship with Christ, that she hadn't previously realized existed.

"It has to do with commitment, Sue. You have to submit your will to the will of God and invite Jesus to be the Lord of your life."

"Yeah, well, the only way I'd be ready to do that is under some sort of contract."

"Contract? What do you mean?"

"For instance, where I'd have to go," Sue answered. "I definitely would not be willing to go to Africa as a missionary. And what I'd have to give up. I love playing cards, especially bridge, and I'm certainly not ready to give that up. I'd want a contract with God as some kind of safety net before I'd be ready to submit that completely."

They laughed gently, tolerantly. "Sorry, Sue. It just doesn't work that way. You're still trying to retain control."

There was no pressure. Many of them were seeking as she was. Together every week, they studied their Bibles, prayed for each other, and gradually grew in their faith. With no fanfare, no flashes of lightning or ringing of bells, Sue gradually committed more and more of her life to Christ. She came to understand *that* as essential; with only the saving knowledge of Jesus Christ, Christians are really quite incomplete.

During these months of growth, she learned about the Order of St. Luke, a group of Christians who practiced a healing ministry. They had named their organization for the writer of the third Gospel, Luke, the physician. They claimed to heal people through prayer and the "laying on of hands." Sue distrusted their claims. She did not believe God was in the miracle business in the twentieth century.

She also heard about Faith at Work, a non-denominational, nation-wide organization of Christians who cultivate a personal relationship with God and an open, sharing relationship with the "significant others" in their lives. Faith at Work held a regional conference in the First Presbyterian Church of Royal Oak in 1965. The conference was not sponsored by the church; they merely had permission to use the facilities.

Several members of Sue's prayer group were involved in the conference, especially in providing weekend housing for the teams of leaders from out of town. When Sue was asked to make their guest room available, she hesitated.

"Maybe you'd like to host someone from the Order of St. Luke, for Larry's benefit," someone suggested.

"No!" she exclaimed. "I don't want anyone 'laying hands' on Larry! We'll take a couple, but only on the condition that they're not from the Order of St. Luke.

*Bill's not going to like this, but there's really no reason
we can't have a couple stay at our house. And this way, maybe
he'll go to some of the meetings with me.*

"Bill, I agreed to make our guest room available to a couple for the Faith At Work Conference weekend," she said
quickly, gingerly.

"You *what*?"

"A couple from Faith At Work will be staying here next
weekend."

"Who are they?"

"I don't know yet. We'll find out Friday night at the conference."

Bill's thin lips disappeared into his mouth as he clamped
his jaws together. His eyes were grim. Although he was silent,
Sue got the message of his disapproval.

*It's bad enough she didn't ask me ahead of time, but worse,
these will be total strangers. Not even the members of the
prayer group know who's staying where yet. Well, I'm certainly not going to let some religious freaks pressure me into
saying or doing anything I'm not sure I want to do. I won't
even go to the meetings if I don't want to. Probably be like
the tent-meeting revivals back home.*

But when Friday night came, a combination of curiosity
and hospitality brought Bill with Sue to the opening session
of the conference. At the registration table in Fellowship Hall,
they picked up name tags, a schedule, and their small group
assignments. They were surprised to see people enthusiastically hugging each other in greeting—women hugging each other,
women hugging men, even men hugging men! The surroundings of the building itself were familiar, but Bill and Sue had
never seen anything like this infectious joy in their church.
They went on into the sanctuary.

From the lectern, John Dutton, the area director of Faith at Work, welcomed everyone. He introduced the song leader, and soon the formal hall rang out with songs of praise. Then Mr. Dutton called on a young man in the audience to come forward and tell how God had been at work in his life lately. This young man walked briskly down the aisle, took the microphone, and told his story. He was followed by an older woman and then a teenager. They didn't talk about conversion experiences but about how God had met their needs in seemingly impossible situations and how they had grown in their faith and in their ability to give God credit for His mighty works. Bill and Sue listened intently, amazed that ordinary people could speak so freely about their faith.

The main speaker of the evening, Walter Judd, the Congressman from Minnesota, was introduced. He was dynamic, relating his faith to his work in government.

The song leader taught them a chorus of reverent petition and praise, and then they were sent to small groups for discussion and closing prayers. Bill and Sue were assigned to different groups.

In the discussion groups of ten or twelve people, one couple had been trained for leadership. They asked each member to introduce himself by name, occupation, and family and then briefly tell what he considered "the growing edge" in his life—the point at which God was leading him to new understanding or commitment. In their separate small groups of strangers, both Bill and Sue heard stories of business failures, struggles with alcoholism, and marital problems. Their problems with Larry seemed almost simple by comparison. They found themselves caring deeply for these people who had been so open. The small group meetings ended with prayers for the participants and for the weekend conference.

During the social hour that followed, the Pattons met their guests, Barbara and Bucky Lippitt from Wisconsin. Later the

Lippitts followed the Pattons home.

The four of them sat at the round dinette table, drinking coffee and getting acquainted.

"I'm a plumber, own my own firm," Bucky announced. "Since the Lord came into my life a few years ago, I've turned the business over to Him. I go into someone's home to fix a leaky pipe, say, and maybe the man of the house hangs around talking to me while I work. So I tell him about the Lord. I witness to people in their own homes. While I work on their plumbing, the Lord works on them. It works out fine. What do you do, Bill?"

"I teach physical education at an elementary school in Bloomfield Hills."

"Oh yeah? You must really like kids. We do, too. Have five of our own. How many kids do you have, Sue?"

"Two. Larry is nine and Steve is seven. Larry has cerebral palsy. We're really lucky to be in this area, because the Detroit Orthopaedic Clinic provides the best help he could get anywhere in the country, we're convinced."

Barbara spoke up quietly. "Isn't it wonderful how the Lord meets the needs of His children? One of our little boys had a punctured ear drum. The doctor said it would be a permanent, complete hearing loss in that ear. We were really upset, so we prayed about it and the Lord healed it."

"What do you mean?"

"The eardrum grew back together. The next time that doctor looked at it, there wasn't even a scar where the hole had been. The doctor could hardly believe it. He asked us what had happened. We didn't know *anything* had happened until the doctor told us. We told him we had prayed about it, that was all. Well, the Lord really took care of it. His hearing is fine now."

Bill and Sue looked at each other over their coffee cups and said nothing. Barbara and Bucky's son had apparently been healed. This was the closest they had come to a divine healing. But neither Bill nor Sue wanted to pursue that topic.

The conversation continued about the Faith At Work conference and the marvelous things they had heard. When the coffee pot was empty and the clock said twelve-thirty, someone suggested it was time for bed.

"Before we break this up, let's have a prayer together," Bucky suggested. And they did, each of the four in turn praying aloud, thanking God for their new friendship and the way He was working in the lives of so many people. It was the first time in their marriage that Bill and Sue had prayed aloud together.

The next morning Bill refused to attend the conference.

"I've got too much work to do here at home," he said. "Besides, that's an awful lot of babysitting for one weekend."

"But I've already arranged for a babysitter," Sue protested.

"Then cancel her. I'm staying home."

Sue was dismayed but knew better than to argue. "Will you come to the night session? Walter Judd is speaking again."

"I might."

"*Might?* What'll I tell the babysitter?"

"Tell her you *might* need her tonight!"

So Sue went on to the conference with Barbara and Bucky.

When Bill has a lot on his mind, he works hard physically. That day he cleaned out the garage, something he'd been putting off for weeks. As he moved bikes and lawnmower, rakes and tires, out into the driveway, he thought through what he had seen and heard the night before. He hosed out the garage and put everything back neatly. It was only eleven o'clock.

He went in where the boys were watching cartoons on TV and made a cup of coffee. The scenes from last night still replayed in his head. He couldn't sit still. Restlessly he wandered down to the basement and began straightening his workbench.

By two-thirty the whole basement was tidy and clean. His mind refused to shut off. These were ordinary people like him and Sue, not "professional Christians." They hurt, and God was active in their lives. And they were joyful about it. Bill began washing windows.

At church, Sue listened to the morning speaker and then attended a workshop on Growth in the Faith. After lunch there was a time for group singing and then a workshop on prayer. It was a heavy dose of what she had been learning in her weekly prayer group: God wants you to commit more and more of your life to Him. As you grow in your faith, He will show you what aspects of your life need to be improved, and when you ask Him to, He will help you in those areas.

Sue heard couples discussing their marital relationships and how God had brought them closer together. One young man said, "This may not sound like much, but I'm a very neat person, and my wife, Judy, just *isn't*. She was driving me crazy with little things, like, believe it or not, it really irritated me that she squeezed the toothpaste tube in the middle instead of rolling it up tight from the end. I asked her not to, but she kept forgetting. It was getting to be a real hassle between us. And finally the Lord let me know that it wasn't all that important and that I needed Judy's carelessness to balance my neatness. So now Judy sometimes rolls the tube up right and sometimes she forgets. When I see it squeezed in the middle, I don't get upset anymore—I just thank God for Judy and what she means to me and for the way He is helping us grow in our marriage."

During the appreciative laughter that followed that account, Sue thought, *I wish Bill and I shared together like that. I've been growing in my faith through the prayer group, but I don't know where he is. I want Bill and me to be on the same level in our Christian growth.* In the second meeting of the discussion group she had met with the night before, she asked them to pray that she and Bill would grow together in their commitment to God.

Bill did go to the Saturday night session, ostensibly just to hear Walter Judd. Following the discussion groups, Sue and the Lippitts wanted to go out for coffee with some friends from the conference, but Bill had had enough. His mind was too full for more conversation. He told Sue to go ahead with Barbara and Bucky. He would go home and dismiss the babysitter.

Bill went home upset. He felt cornered, pushed. He didn't want to talk to Barbara and Bucky that night as they had the night before. He was afraid, afraid they would push him for some kind of commitment. From what he had seen of Bucky, Bill didn't think his silent routine would hold. Bucky would not let him just not answer. He would push.

When the Lippitts and Sue pulled into the driveway, they sat in the car talking for a few minutes. Sue had realized many things about herself and her relationship with Bill that day, insights that so far she hadn't verbalized.

In the car, Bucky said in his abrupt way, "What do we want here tonight?"

Sue answered, "I'd like for Bill and me to make a full commitment of our lives to God. I feel like I've committed some aspects, but we're not together in this. We haven't even talked about it."

"Okay, let's just ask Him about it now. Lord, go with us into this house. Be present as the four of us talk together tonight. Open Bill's heart, and let all four of us be open to Your leading, whatever that might be. Amen."

At that point, Bill came to the door to say that Bucky had a phone call, so all of them went in. In a few minutes, they were comfortably seated in the living room, Barbara and Sue on the couch, Bucky in Bill's big chair, Bill in the rocker. Sue began to tell them what she had discovered about herself that day. Her voice rose and fell, sometimes excited, sometimes tender, sometimes choked with emotion.

"I've realized today what a selfish wife I've been. All my relationship with Bill depended on what he did for me. If he remembered my birthday, Mother's Day, Valentine's Day, and our anniversary with the appropriate gifts and romance, then I'd love him. I've wanted him to put me first, and I've never given much thought at all to putting him first or what his needs are or what I should be doing for him."

The three looked at Bill to see his reaction to this startling confession. He sat uncomfortably gripping the arms of the rocking chair, not meeting their eyes.

Sue continued, "My love has been very conditional. I realize I need to change all this. I've been operating from a base of insecurity. I haven't had enough confidence in myself to believe that Bill would stay with me, that we would be a happily married couple forever and forever. Because of that guy in college who broke off the engagement with me the year before you came, Bill, I guess I've always felt that some-day you'd leave me, and I didn't want to be vulnerable. I didn't want to love you in a way that might hurt me later. So I've nagged and nagged. I've not trusted your decisions. I guess I felt that if I held the upper hand, I was protected if you left. I could sort of say, 'Who needs him anyway?'"

Again Bill felt their eyes upon him. His eyes lowered, his knuckles white on the brown arms of the rocker, he still said nothing. *She's right*, he thought. *She has given me a rough way to go. I'm glad she's realized it, but it hasn't really been as bad as she says. How awful for her to have to spill her guts like this in front of other people!*

Sue, Barbara, and Bucky waited for some response from him. It would have been a perfect time for a declaration of love. Bill remained silent.

"What do you think, Bill?" Bucky questioned.

Bill glanced up shyly. "In my family, when you get married, that's it. Divorce is never an option," he said softly.

Nothing was said for a while as his words and all their implications sank in.

Then Sue went on, "In our weekly prayer group, we've been talking about letting Christ be Lord of our lives, not just our Savior. Bill and I are both Christians. We believe Christ died for our sins, and we are certainly active in church. But we've never really committed our lives to Him and consulted Him about decisions and so on. I'd like to do that, but I think we should do it together. I want Bill and me to be on the same level in our Christian walk."

The spindles of the rocker were like prison bars against Bill's back. He carefully sealed himself behind a wall of silence. They waited.

Finally Barbara said, "It's very late. Maybe we should go to bed."

"The Lord's work isn't done yet," Bucky retorted.

"Well," Barbara suggested, "maybe we should pray and see if there's something blocking Bill."

Dimly Bill heard their voices. He was hearing other voices, too, voices from his childhood.

"Hey, Billy, you hit the sawdust trail last night, didn't you?"

"Boy, you was cryin' like a baby! You musta been quite a sinner!"

"How come you never let us in on any of that fun, Billy? All we got out of it was seein' you actin' like a bawl-baby in fronta that evangelist!"

Surrounded by taunting classmates, Bill had quickly built a fragile wall of silence around his emotions, a wall which grew higher, wider, and thicker with each year, with each hurt, with each putdown. And now his wife and these new friends, and even Christ himself, were chipping and chiseling away his fortress that had become his prison.

Tears welled up in his eyes, and Bill finally broke his silence. "I've always been afraid to show my emotions. When I was a kid, I was teased for going forward at a tent meeting. My family always has been uncomfortable with any emotionalism."

"It's okay to show your feelings, Bill," Bucky told him. "It's only human to cry. If you bottle up your feelings, it hurts inside and you can't relate to people very well. I used to be that way, too, before the Lord came into my life."

Now the tears streamed down Bill's cheeks.

"Are you ready now to commit your life to the Lord, Bill?" Bucky persisted.

No answer.

Finally, half exasperated, Bucky said, "Do you want to accept the Lord or not?"

Suddenly for Bill it was no longer "Are you ready?" It was a matter of acceptance or rejection. So he nodded dumbly.

"Great! Let's pray." Bucky's voice was triumphant. "Lord, here are Bill and Sue to commit their lives to You."

"Dear Lord, I'm sorry for the way I've treated Bill and for my lack of trust in him. Bill and I want You to be the Lord of our lives, not just our Savior. We promise to ask what You want in all situations of our life together. Thank you, Lord," Sue murmured.

"O God, forgive me for holding back. I want You to be the Lord of our life."

"Thank you, Father, for these friends," Barbara prayed. "Thank You for their commitment. Hold them fast in Your love."

Bucky concluded the prayer, and they opened their eyes. The room was thick with the loving presence of Christ. It was so real to all of them that they could nearly see Jesus standing in their midst.

The floodgates of Bill's emotions were wide open, and the

tears gushed forth for several hours. Years of hurts, disappointments, and fears that had been dammed up so effectively now poured out.

The next morning the Lippitts went with the Patton family to the regular Sunday morning worship service and then back to church that afternoon for the final session of the Faith At Work conference. The concluding part was a time for the participants to share with the whole conference how God had worked in their lives during this special weekend. Sue told about their new commitment to make Christ the Lord of their lives. Bill would have spoken, for both of them, but he was still crying!

From then on, Bill and Sue studied the Scriptures and prayed, but not much seemed to change. Six months after the conference, John Dutton, the area Faith At Work director, met with Pattons and another couple. All four expressed a sense of let-down after the spiritual mountain-top of the conference.

"You need to be in a group together," he told them. "Some of us from the city will come out to meet with you for Bible study, prayer, and fellowship. Invite your friends, and when your group has grown enough in size and spirit, you'll be ready to go on without us."

That was the take-off point for Bill and Sue's growth together in their Christian faith. Sue continued to attend the weekly prayer group at church, as well. They began to learn what kind of God they had accepted, a God who loved them so much that all His riches were at their disposal.

Their Bible study was about the life of Jesus and the promises of the Christian faith. It was not primarily a study of miracles in general or healing in particular. But as they dug into the Gospels with their friends, they encountered stories about the physical healings that Christ performed. Gradually they began to ask themselves if God might heal Larry.

At an area evangelistic meeting Sue attended with members of her weekly prayer group, the leader asked for prayer requests for those who needed healing. Sue decided to "test the waters" by praying for her dad, who had diabetes. There was no miraculous healing, but his condition did improve.

What did that mean? If her faith had been stronger, would a miracle have occurred? Was there a formula she hadn't learned yet? Or was her dad's improvement merely coincidental?

Reading Christian books and listening to others' experiences, Sue and Bill learned more about how big and wonderful God is, that He is able to do anything, willing to give the best He has and withhold nothing that would be good for them. Their faith and understanding increased.

In the summer of 1966, Eunice Bitzer told the prayer group that she would be attending Camp Farthest Out, a Christian camp with nationally known leaders. She invited the rest of them to come along, if not for the whole week at least for a day or two.

Sue and her friend Margaret decided to go for two days in the middle of the week. Eunice was delighted to see them. When it was time for them to leave, she asked if they would like one of the leaders, Tommy Tyson, to pray with them for a special blessing. This was not an unusual opportunity Eunice was offering them. CFO leaders are usually available for prayer with those who must leave before the concluding blessing service.

Sue and Margaret accepted rather diffidently. It was apparent that Eunice thought this was something they should do. But what blessing should they ask Tyson to pray for?

Eunice escorted them back-stage in the auditorium. "Tommy, I'd like you to meet Sue and Margaret. They've come up from my church for only a couple of days, and now they're about to leave. I wondered if you would pray for a special blessing for each of them."

"Sure," he answered, beaming and shaking hands firmly with them. "What shall we pray for?"

"I'd like to ask God to make me a better wife and mother," Sue said, having decided that would be a safe enough request.

Tyson searched her face. "Okay," he said, a bit uncertainly. "You have a problem at home, right? You have two children—girls?"

Sue looked at him amazed. "No, boys," she replied. Had Eunice told him about her family, about Larry, she wondered. Yet, somehow, she knew that was not the case. Tyson was tuned in to the Holy Spirit.

He placed his hands on her head and prayed hesitantly, feeling for words, listening to the Holy Spirit. And Sue began to think, *I'd better be honest with God now or I'll regret it the rest of my life.*

When he finally said amen and opened his eyes to look at her again, Sue said, "Tommy, I think maybe I've asked for the wrong thing. My son Larry is ten years old and has cerebral palsy. Would you pray for his healing, with me as proxy?" She had seen evangelists pray for healing of a third party by laying hands on the one who requested the prayers. It took a lot of courage to make this step, but she had the growing conviction that if she didn't, she would be making a dreadful mistake.

"Of course," he said simply. With his hands on her head again, this time he prayed, with real conviction, for Larry's healing.

At that moment, God took the burden of Larry's problem away from her, a tremendous load off her back. God said, "I'll take care of it." *Sue* received the healing because she knew from that moment on she could trust Jesus. Never again would she experience the awful burden of worrying about what would happen to her child. She knew he was in God's hands and God would look after him.

When Tommy Tyson finished, Sue began to cry. She cried for a long time. As Margaret drove her home, she wondered if Larry would have experienced a miraculous healing. She envisioned the excitement, wonder, and joy that might have occurred at the moment of Tyson's prayer. What would Larry look like?

Yet deep within her, she knew that Larry would be unchanged. It was *she* who had been healed, not Larry. This was a blessing she had never thought to request—the blessing of being able to trust God completely to do what was best for Larry, the blessing of being relieved of the total responsibility for the future. He was in God's hands, and God would look after him! She could hardly wait to tell Bill.

Grandfather and Grandmother Patton, Grandmother and Grandfather Wall, on the day Larry was baptized, March 25, 1956.

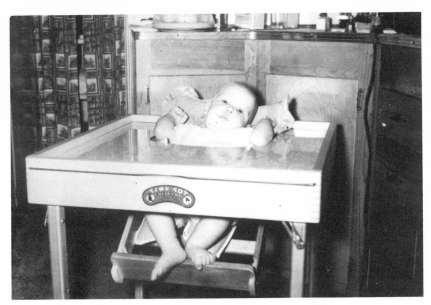

Larry at 4 months (1956) in the trailer, seated at the table used for eating and play.

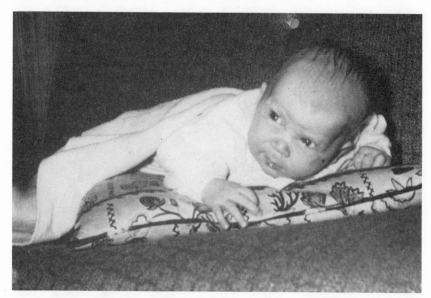

Larry at 6 months in trailer, Hanover College, mid-February, 1956.

Larry at 10 months: A happy boy in his Taylor Tot.

Mother and Dad Patton, Bill and Larry at Bill's graduation, Hanover College, Indiana, June 1957.

Larry at 14 months, at Royal Oak apartment, with Taylor Tot used as a walker.

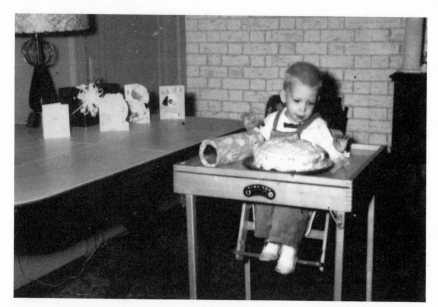

Larry, 2 years, January 11, 1958. This is the table Larry ate and played in, at the Royal Oak apartment.

Larry (2¾ years), Mother, Stevie (1 year), on his birthday, November 10, 1958.

Ruth and Wallace Foster with Stevie (1 year) and Larry (2 years), Easter, 1958.

Detroit Orthopaedic Clinic (now Detroit Institute for Children), new building, 1959-1960. Larry started going weekly, then 3 mornings a week, to D.O.C. in January 1958, then to Nursery School from February 1959—September 7, 1960.

Larry (4½), Aunt Judy (Sue's sister), Steve (2¾), August 21, 1960, First Presbyterian Church. Larry's short leg braces can hardly be seen.

Stevie (4 years) and Larry (5½ years) on November 24, 1961. Larry is wearing the helmet he hated over his hat.

Donna Weathers, Lynn Galliger, Chris McCue, Peter Hassey, Larry Patton (striped shirt), Debbie Zinser, October 1965. "Work at Tyler Orthopedic Unit."

Larry (7) and Steve (5) on October 20, 1962.

Larry, orthopedic unit, Tyler Elementary School (now Avery Elementary School).

Larry, Cub Scout.

Larry in Scout uniform.

D-A Boy Scout Camp, 1968.

D-A Boy Scout Camp awards night. Larry won an award for biggest fish caught (1968).

Pattons try out camping with Fosters at Burt Lake, Michigan, 1967. Neal Foster, Larry, Steve, Wallace Foster (seated), Ruth Foster, Sue.

Steve, Stephanie, Grandma and Grandpa Wall, Jenny, Larry, on the Walls' 60th anniversary, March 1988.

Larry's friends from Tyler Orthopedic Unit help him celebrate his 13th birthday (1-11-69). "Happy birthday, Larry."

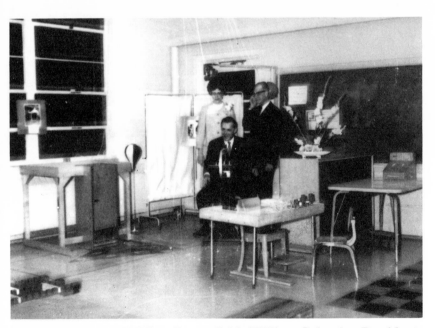

Sue, Congressman William Broomfield, William Calverly - President, Exchange Club, October 17, 1965, at Tyler Parents Orthopedic Group reception.

After the Soap Box Derby, 1968, Larry still likes cars.

Disneyland, California, the summer of 1971.

Steve guarded by Larry. Hoosiers at heart, Michigan basketball.

1968 - "Watermelon time at D-A Boy Scout camp. Steve seated on bench on left, Larry right behind Steve's right shoulder, Dick Stratton in upper right. He made it possible for Larry to go to camp.

Steve, Larry, Sue, Bill on June 13, 1971, at First Presbyterian Church. Larry received God and Country award for Boy Scouts.

9

"The Doctors' Walk"

In September, 1966, Larry sat next to his parents on the long, hard bench in the hall of the D.O.C. It was time for his six month check-up. While Dad turned pages of a magazine and Mom talked to other mothers, Larry watched the children out of the corner of his eye. He hated it when people stared at him, so he was careful not to be obvious.

Several children were confined to their individually designed wheelchairs with padded head rests and Velcro straps. Others wore short braces buckled securely under their knees and fastened to ugly, high-topped brown leather oxfords. Larry hadn't had to wear braces for two years now. What a relief it had been to leave them off! The other children's padded helmets, like his, were sweaty and smelly. How he hated his helmet! It was the first thing he yanked off as he came through the front door at home after school.

A kid about Larry's size lurched along on crutches, dragging his legs encased in steel and leather. *I'm not as bad as he is*, Larry told himself.

This was the reason he observed the others so surreptitiously, to measure himself against them. He knew he had to have therapy and wear a helmet and had had to wear braces. He knew he wasn't as strong as other kids and couldn't defend himself. He knew he had trouble walking and talking. But so what? He was just a regular kid who hated homework and couldn't wait to go out to play with the rest of the neighborhood gang. All the therapy and hardware only emphasized his differentness and interrupted his fun. He wanted to hurry through all this and get home in time to play whiffle ball in the street with Steve and Dave, Mark and Herb.

From his seat in the lobby, Larry could see the D.O.C. courtyard laid out like a miniature city. Concrete paths intersected, and bushes and a small fountain completed the landscaping. Tiny children from the D.O.C. nursery school rode tricycles or pedal cars, obeying stop and yield signs.

He remembered what a relief it had been, after what seemed like hours of therapy, to pedal a trike along those small streets, drag racing another kid to an intersection, screeching enthusiastically as he slammed on the brakes, leaving a trio of tire marks on the white pavement at the stop sign. Then all too soon he would be called back in for more therapy.

Watching these children today, Larry yawned. It was super getting to miss school, but he didn't like getting up so early. There were no appointments at D.O.C. Doctors took people on a first-come, first-serve basis, so Mom and Dad always wanted to get there early. Usually they were back at school by 10 or 10:30, so Larry tried to talk them into stopping at McDonalds or doing errands to prolong going back to school. Sometimes it worked.

They sat in the hallway waiting, like a lottery. Even after the receptionist called out, "Patton, for Dr. LaMont," there was more waiting, this time in chairs outside the doctor's examining room. There Larry could keep track of who was next.

Finally a white-uniformed young woman came out with his file folder and said, "Larry Patton? This way please."

Mom or Dad took him back to the dressing room area, picked up a stiff white cotton gown from the attendant, and went into a dressing room where Larry struggled to change clothes.

He hated the stupid gowns. Why did he have to wear them, anyway? All he had to do was walk across the stupid floor, so why did he have to wear the stupid gown? Terri timed him dressing and undressing himself at school, and he hated that, too. It was embarrassing. *Why don't you have to do this, too?* he thought.

Dr. LaMont, Larry's orthopedic doctor, was in the examining room along with a couple of residents, therapists, and Mrs. Chapin, the social worker assigned to the Pattons.

Dr. LaMont took charge. "How're you doing today, Larry?"

"Fine."

"How's school going?"

"Fine."

Half-turning to Bill and Sue, Dr. LaMont checked it out. "Is he really doing fine at school?"

"Seems to be."

"Good! Now, Larry, walk from this corner to that one for me."

Larry's bare feet padded on the cold tiles, sticking slightly as he angled diagonally across the room.

"Hmm. Still toeing in quite a lot. Okay, thank you, Larry. You can get dressed now."

Happily, Larry hurried back to the dressing room, ripped off the stupid gown and wrestled himself into his clothes again. He did not hear the conversation between the doctors and his parents.

On the way home, Larry was surprised that his parents agreed to stop at McDonalds. He didn't even have to talk them into it! As he struggled with his hamburger, french fries, and drink, he tried to balance the time. He loved the treat so much that he wanted to wolf it down, but he also wanted to stall so he wouldn't have to go back to school yet. He concentrated so hard that he missed most of what Mom and Dad said to each other. He did catch something about moving his bed and another snatch about a remote control from Grand-pa Wall.

Later, in the car, Larry wondered about what he had overheard. Where were they going to move his bed? It had been only a year or so ago that Larry and Steve had been moved upstairs. That big finished attic room had been for-bidden territory. It was Dad's study while he worked on his master's degree. Larry had been awed by the importance and loftiness of that space. Then Dad had graduated, and sud-denly he and Steve had been moved up there.

The bedroom upstairs seemed much farther away. Larry hated the stairs. Mom always wanted him and Steve to keep their things in their room, but he just tossed his stuff on the stairs instead of making extra trips up and down. In the morn-ings he always threw his clothes over the rail and then got dressed sitting on the bottom step. Sometimes he came downstairs sitting down, sometimes head first. Mom always fussed. It was better exercise to walk down, she kept saying. He didn't care. The stairs were an obstacle course that slowed him down. He would deal with them in the quickest, easiest way. Maybe now the folks were ready to let him move back downstairs.

Larry grabbed the back of the front seat and pulled himself forward. "You gonna move my bed, Mom?"

"Dr. LaMont is concerned about your toeing in," she began. "He thinks maybe there's something they can do about it." She hesitated.

What's this got to do with moving my bed? Larry wondered.

"They're considering operating on your legs to turn those bones enough that your feet will go straight . . ."

Larry burst into tears. "No way!" he cried. "They're not gonna cut on me!"

"It wouldn't be till next summer, Larry" Sue tried to soothe him. "We would move your bed down to the TV room, and maybe Grandpa Wall would let you use his remote control gadget for a few months."

Larry howled in panic. "Next summer! A few months! No way!" He would miss the six weeks summer program at school. He would miss out on all the whiffle ball and the arguments he enjoyed provoking, knowing Steve would fight for him. He wouldn't be able to throw the ball at the strike zone he had drawn on the garage door so he could practice to be a major league pitcher. He couldn't bike down to the A & W stand for a 25 cent root beer on hot evenings. No way!

Suddenly Dad's firm voice cut through his hysteria. "Cool it, Larry. They haven't *decided*. They just mentioned it as a possibility. They'll make up their minds in June. So just calm down."

It took the usual half-hour for Larry to recover from this upsetting news. *No way*, he kept telling himself. *I'm gonna work really hard in therapy, and they're gonna be so impressed that they'll leave me alone.* Mom gave him tissues to blow his nose and helped him pull himself together by the time they got back to school.

Larry's intentions were good, but June was a long time off from September. In his involvement with Cub Scouts, children's choir at church, neighborhood play, and of course homework, he lost patience with therapy. *I'm doing fine*, he thought. *Those doctors won't operate.*

In January, Dr. Lamont recommended short leg braces again. Now that he was growing pretty fast, maybe braces would straighten that toeing-in. *Fine*, Larry thought. *Braces are a bother, but surely now I won't have to have the operation.*

Braces again! He's getting worse instead of better! Sue was devastated by the decision. This made her more determined than ever that the surgery should take place. Larry's gait was bad enough, and the grimaces that twisted his face. But now braces again. They were so ugly and so noisy. Why did Larry's handicap have to be so noticeable? She asked her prayer group to pray that the right decision would be made and that she would be able to accept the Lord's will for Larry and for her.

Bill was opposed to the operation from the beginning. He had taken enough anatomy and human physiology classes to be convinced that the surgical procedure would not accomplish what the doctor expected and might even make matters worse. He could not understand Sue's eagerness for it.

On June 28, 1967, there was a clinical consultation at D.O.C. to decide on a dirotation of the left femur. X-rays of Larry's legs and feet were stuck on light panels. Dr. Lamont, Dr. Frederick Fisher, the head of the orthopedic surgeons for the clinic, therapists, social workers, interns, and Mom and Dad watched as Larry made the diagonal, barefoot walk that might determine the rest of the summer.

He had been revving himself up for this walk for about two weeks. Now he concentrated harder than he ever had before. It helped to be barefoot. He was aware of how every square centimeter of skin was meeting the cool tiles: back edge of left heel, full heel, arch, instep, ball, little toe, next toe, next, next, big toe, then forward to right heel. It seemed to take the whole summer to cross the room and return, with everyone staring silently. Then the Pattons were excused to change Larry's clothes and sit in the waiting room while the doctors decided his future.

Another summer seemed to go by while they waited. Finally Mrs. Chapin came for them. "Make an appointment for next week. Dr. LaMont will talk to you then," she reported.

"What was their decision?" Sue anxiously inquired.

"What did they say? Do I have to have the operation?"

"They'll decide next week."

"Next week!" Larry was outraged. He had waited all that time, and now they wouldn't decide until *next week! Oh, well,* he consoled himself, *that's at least seven more days of freedom!*

Sue managed to keep her composure while they took Larry to a playground for his team's scheduled game in the Berkley Department of Recreation Baseball League. Then she drove Bill to work. He was teaching drivers' education for the summer. She struggled to hold the tears back until both of them were out of the car. Then, as tears spilled down her cheeks, she headed for the church to find her friend, Kathie Irwin. Kathie, seeing how upset Sue was, took her to a small lounge where they could talk alone.

As the door closed, Sue burst into loud, racking sobs. "Why didn't God answer our prayers? I went to the clinic fully expecting to take Larry right to Children's Hospital to be admitted. I even asked Bill if we should pack Larry a bag. He said no, but I still thought . . ." She couldn't continue because of the tears.

Kathie listened patiently, offered Sue a tissue, and tried to find words of comfort. Then she suggested they pray together.

As they did, it was as though God reminded Sue she had trusted Him for six months for an answer. Was it really so difficult to wait one more week?

Reassured, at least for the moment, Sue thanked Kathie with a hug and drove home—to wait.

During that week when Larry tried not to think about the possibility of surgery, Sue thought of nothing else. She had everyone praying that the right decision would be made. Then Betty Farah called. "I know the decision about surgery for

Larry is for you and the doctors to make, but I feel compelled to say this. Larry has done well this year and gained so much. A whole summer of immobility would probably set him back at least a year in what we try to accomplish with him at school. In addition, I am not at all sure the results will be what you hope. Larry may not be able to walk as well after surgery as he can now. Forgive me for intruding my opinion, but I thought you ought to have this input."

On July 5, Bill and Sue met Dr. LaMont at the D.O.C. for the final conference. They listened again as he spelled out the procedure, which he carefully labeled "optional."

With the call from Betty in her head, the full realization of Bill's opposition to the surgery, and the awareness of everyone's prayers upholding them, Sue asked, "Dr. LaMont, if Larry were your son, what would you do?"

After a brief silence, Dr. LaMont said, "If he were my son, I would not choose surgery."

Bill and Sue looked at each other. Both of them recognized this was God's answer to their many prayers. It was crystal clear. Bill raised an eyebrow and shrugged.

"That's it, then. No surgery." Sue pushed her glasses back up and got ready to leave, but Dr. LaMont wasn't finished.

"Since he's doing so well, let's take off the braces and let him wear normal shoes for the summer. And I'd like to see him again in October."

When Larry heard the verdict of no surgery, he was jubilant. He had just been given back his whole summer. But he didn't realize that this meant he would *never* have the surgery. So every six months, he walked carefully and beautifully for the doctors, hoping against hope they would not sentence him to surgery. No one knew of his misconception. His teachers teased him about walking so much better for the doctors than he did on a daily basis. They referred to it as Larry's "doctors' walk."

10

Scouting and Bikes

The car door opened in the driveway and Larry and Steve piled out of the back seat. Steve gave a shrill whistle to call the other kids over, and before Bill had put the car away and gone inside, the whiffle-ball game was beginning.

"How was Scouts tonight?" Sue asked as she poured Bill a glass of iced tea.

Bill blew his nose before answering and then took a gulp of the cold drink. "Fine," he responded, but his voice sounded funny. Sue finally looked at him. His eyes were red-rimmed.

"What happened?" she asked.

"You know Dick Stratton, the Boy Scout area exec? He came up to me this evening and offered to take full responsibility for Larry if we'd let him go to Scout camp this summer." Tears filled Bill's eyes again.

"Why, Bill! He hardly knows us!" Sue exclaimed wonderingly.

"I know. We talked a while about what Larry could and couldn't do, and Dick says Larry's been such a good scout this year that he will be glad to be responsible for him. Says it would be a great experience for Larry and for the other campers to have him there. What do you think?"

"It would," she stammered, her own eyes brimming. "Bill, this is the first time anyone except my family and the Fosters has ever offered to be responsible for him for any length of time! Does Larry want to go?"

"You should have seen his face tonight during the movie about Scout camp. I'd say he wants to go."

"Well, God bless Dick Stratton! That's wonderful!"

Later that evening, after Larry had fallen asleep, Steve crept downstairs. Mom and Dad were getting ready for bed.

"Can I talk to you for a while?"

"Sure, Steve. What's on your mind?"

"Larry got the prize for selling ice cream topping for Scouts, and it's not fair!"

"Oh? Why not?"

"We took some to church Sunday to sell, remember? And this one man—I don't know his name—I asked him to buy some, and he said he couldn't afford it. Then later I saw him carrying a jar! I couldn't figure out what had happened, and then Larry came up and told me he'd sold it to him. The guy told *me* he couldn't afford it, but then when he saw Larry, he felt sorry for him and bought some! That's not fair!"

"No, it isn't," Mom admitted. "But I wouldn't get that upset about one jar of topping."

"But, Mom, there was a prize, *money*, for selling the most topping! I put just as much effort into it as Larry, but if people are gonna buy from him because they feel *sorry* for him, I wonder if I ever have a chance!"

"Yeah, Steve," Dad said, "Larry does get a lot of attention because of his handicap. People do buy things from him out of pity sometimes or because they admire his efforts to overcome the CP. And Larry probably realizes that. I bet he would be glad to give up all that attention if he could get rid of the handicap. Don't you think so?"

"Yeah, prob'ly."

"You get attention, too, Steve, for things Larry can never do, things like sports, and music. He'd never be able to play the clarinet the way you do," Mom pointed out.

Steve began to feel better.

"Not only that," Bill added, "seeing you do so well at something makes him try harder. He might not have learned to play ball so well if he hadn't been trying to keep up with you."

By this time Steve was smiling again. He was proud of Larry's accomplishments, and if he had had a part in them, he was glad.

After he had gone back to bed, his parents talked about it some more.

"Poor Steve," Sue said, "Larry does get lots of attention, and most people don't think Steve needs any."

"The competition between them has always been strong, from the time Steve was born."

"Yes. It's been good for Larry, but Steve has kind of come out on the short end. Remember when my mother was bragging on Larry for trying to tie his shoes, and Steve said, 'Look, Grandma. I can tie my shoes!' No one ever thought to praise him for his accomplishments because of course he could do them. But every little thing Larry has mastered has been a big deal."

"Well, I think Steve's going to be all right. He's proud of Larry and looks out for him with the neighborhood kids."

"Won't it be great for Steve to be the only child while Larry is at Scout Camp! He'll enjoy that as much as Larry will enjoy camp! Thank goodness for Dick Stratton!"

The campfire blazed higher. Behind the leaders and scouts the current of the lake gently tilted the canoe beached on the edge of the clearing. Before them the crowd of parents seated on the hill faded in and out as the flames rose and fell. In the far distance, a full moon was rising behind old Baldy. An older scout in full Indian dress and warpaint pounded louder and faster on the well-worn tom-tom. Suddenly he stopped. As the echoes of the drum-beats faded, the only sounds were crickets, tree-frogs, and the crackle of the campfire.

A shiver of excitement rippled down Larry's spine as he sat cross-legged with the other Scouts. What a fantastic week! The first night had been a little scary, being away from home, but Mr. Stratton was there if he needed him. It had been really neat the way Mr. Stratton had been there but hadn't helped unless Larry really needed him. The other scouts, too, had accepted him without making a big deal about it.

Hiking up Old Baldy and back! What a thrill! He had scrambled to keep up and had only skinned his knees a couple of times. No worse than an ordinary evening of whiffleball!

Dad had come up for a day, same as lots of other dads, but Larry had been so busy he hadn't really thought much about it. The cookies Mom had sent along were gone before he knew it when his patrol found out about them.

Now here it was the closing ceremony. The camp director stood up with lots of papers in his hands. Larry knew it was time for awards, and he hoped his patrol would get at least one. *We should,* he thought. *We're the best!*

After a few preliminary remarks to the parents about what a fine week it had been and some allusions to inside jokes for the scouts' benefit, the director began presenting awards. "The Fisherman of the Week Award goes to a young man who landed a bass 19.5 inches long. That is pretty good! Larry Patton!"

Amid the cheers and applause, Larry scrambled to his feet. He was proud of his accomplishment, but it wasn't the most unusual experience of the week for him. He had caught fish before, maybe not quite that big, but horseback riding had been a first. As he returned with his award to his seat, he remembered what had happened.

The riding instructor had thought Larry should go riding. "Ever try this before?" he had asked.

Larry had shyly shaken his head. The horse loomed high above him. He was not too crazy about the idea of sitting on top of an animal that big and powerful.

"Tell you what!" the horse guy had proposed. "I'll ride with you. You sit in the saddle, right here, and I'll sit right behind and hold you on. What do you say to that?"

Lots of other scouts were watching, urging him to try it. If the guy would hold him on, it shouldn't be too bad. The horse, though huge, looked friendly and gentle. "Okay," Larry agreed.

Several willing hands boosted him up into the creaky leather saddle. The stirrups were adjusted for his short legs, and his feet felt as if they were sticking straight out. He clutched the saddle horn and tried to keep his balance.

"Steady, there," the horse guy soothed the animal as he mounted behind the saddle. Helpful scouts handed the reins to the instructor.

"Here, Larry," he said. "You hold the reins. The horse knows the trail, so you won't really need to guide him. Pull this one if you want him to turn right, and this one if you want him to go left. If you want him to slow down or stop, pull both reins. Now hold the reins, not the saddle horn. I'll hold you on the horse. Ready? Ged-dap!"

And they were off, at an easy pace. Larry soon lost his fear. He even enjoyed the height, as long as the instructor held him securely.

About half a mile down the trail, the horse got excited and reared. The instructor yelled at Larry to hold on as he himself let go and slid off the horse's back. The horse calmed, and Larry rode on, alone.

The instructor wasn't hurt. He could tell that Larry was doing fine, so he just followed along to be sure the rest of the ride went safely.

As Larry guided the horse back into the corral, the waiting scouts cheered him and jeered the instructor. What a joke! Larry had made it back still on the horse, and the instructor limped along on foot!

Now here at the closing campfire, as the last award was presented, Indian war whoops, whistles, and cheers rang out. Camp was over. What a fantastic week! Larry couldn't wait to come back next year!

It was the summer of '69. Larry had just finished seventh grade.

"Larry, I just can't push you any more!" Sue puffed. "We'll try again tomorrow, okay? One of these days you'll make it, and you'll be riding a two-wheeler as well as Steve. Are you okay?"

Larry scrambled to his feet, checked his knees to see if they were bleeding, and then picked up his bike to walk it home. "Yeah, I'm okay."

For days now, Mom and Dad had tried to help him learn to ride the bike. They had taken turns pushing him down the sidewalk, but no matter how hard they pushed, he couldn't get up enough speed to balance on his own.

He longed for a new bike. He was much too big for the old one with training wheels he'd had for years, but Dad had said, "You're not getting a new one till you learn how to ride the old one without the training wheels." Besides, the other kids were going off without him, on their bikes, jumping curbs and whizzing down the street. He had to learn.

Mom went on into the house, but Larry stayed out in the driveway, thinking hard.

Across the street, a neighbor lady watched from her window. She had watched all week, admiring Larry's courage and persistence and Bill and Sue's patience and endurance. She was ready to turn away when suddenly she looked more intently. What was that child about to do?

Sue had gone in, expecting Larry to be right behind her. When she didn't hear the door, she turned and looked out the bay window toward the driveway. There he stood, still, thinking. Why wasn't he coming in? She folded her arms across the middle of the window frame and rested her chin on her wrists, watching.

They're not pushing me fast enough, Larry was thinking. *If I could just get up enough speed, I could balance.* Then he saw the dip in the driveway, the little ramp from sidewalk to street level. *Maybe that would do it!*

He straddled the bike and pushed himself toward the little ramp.

The slight incline gave him the momentum he needed. Pedaling furiously, he wobbled and teetered, balanced himself, and sailed on down the street!

Farther down the block, Herb and Mark cheered as he caught up with them. He circled and rode back home to do it again.

Tears streamed down Sue's face as she watched, and across the street the neighbor lady swallowed hard and brushed tears away, too. Who ever would have thought he'd be able to do that?!

11

Larry Grows in Faith

The second weekend in September, 1969, along with the other seventh and eighth graders from First Presbyterian Church, Larry attended a retreat led by Kathie Irwin, who had become the director of Christian education.

The retreat had been a lot of fun: singing, study, games, hikes, practical jokes. Now it was Sunday morning, and for worship time Kathie led them to a hillside overlooking a pond. They sat in the grass and sang and prayed. Then Kathie began to speak.

"Once there was a young man about your age who was a real character. In school he hung around with a bunch of kids who weren't at all interested in church. But they went because their parents made them. They used to sit in the back row just to make fun of what was going on."

Her audience snickered self-consciously and stole glances at each other.

"One night when these guys were forced to attend, there was an altar call. One kid said to the rest of them, 'Let's go forward and fake it, just for fun.'

"This particular young man I'm telling you about thought that was a great idea and they would all get a big kick out of it, so he went forward. When he got up to the front of the sanctuary, he realized that none of his friends had come along. He was pushed to his knees up there, and an amazing thing happened. The Lord really anointed him and revealed Himself to him.

"When he went back to his seat, the other guys said, 'Great job! You really conned them!'

"He replied, 'Guys, I didn't fake it. That was the real thing.' And his life was never the same. That young man was my dad."

Larry and his friends were quiet now, no longer looking at each other. Some were plucking blades of grass and chewing on the tender ends. Others watched cotton balls of clouds follow each other across the sky. All listened intently as Kathie continued.

"Now you are about the age he was when he made that commitment. Some of you haven't been much interested in church either. You've been there regularly, but mostly because your parents made you come. This year you're going to be in communicants class to learn what church membership is all about. But joining the church doesn't mean much unless you are willing to give your lives to the Lord. I wonder if you're ready to make that step. Let's pray about it."

As she prayed, Larry remembered his mom saying to him just a few weeks earlier, "Larry, you're getting old enough now to consider making your own commitment of faith. Jesus is more than just a Savior. He wants to be the Lord of your life. You'll have to make some decisions at school about various things, and if you ask Jesus to be Lord of your life, He'll guide you to make the right choices. Dad and I have committed our lives to Him, and we consult Him about all kinds of things."

Now Kathie was saying, "Lord Jesus, in the silence of this moment, here in the beauty of Your creation, look into the hearts of these young people." Then to the kids she said in a soft voice that carried even to the back row, "Are you willing to turn your life over to the Lord? If so, just ask Him, silently, to come into your life."

Eyes squeezed tightly shut, Larry prayed, "Lord, come in. I want you to be my Lord." *Mom will be so happy,* he thought.

For the next year, Larry didn't feel any different than before the retreat. He went through the communicants class with the others and joined the church. He continued to struggle with homework and play ball in the neighborhood. He still provoked quarrels for Steve to fight for him. He made rock jewelry and sold ice cream topping for Scouts and went to the D.O.C. to see the doctor. But he didn't feel any different. He had expected to be zapped or something. He questioned the Lord a lot, but if answers came, Larry didn't recognize them.

The Youth Fellowship of the First Presbyterian Church in Royal Oak was a large group. Five couples served as advisors, along with the assistant minister. Several of these adults were also involved in the Saturday night Faith at Work/Bible study group with Bill and Sue.

In 1970 Bill first prayed for Larry's healing. At that point Sue knew that they were ready to go together as a family to a healing service. Then Bill and Sue were invited to participate as team leaders at the Faith At Work Conference, led by Pastor Don Bartow, in Findlay, Ohio. There was a section for teenagers, so it would be appropriate to take Larry and Steve. And there would be a healing service.

The week before the conference, Sue and Bill met with their Saturday night group and told them, "We believe in healing, and we're going to this conference expecting a miracle, that God will heal Larry instantaneously and he will no longer have CP. The healing service will be Saturday afternoon. Please pray for us during that time."

She also told Tom Kirkman, the senior minister, about their plans.

Tom protested, "But what will happen to your faith if God

chooses not to heal Larry instantaneously?"

"We trust God and we know He will do the best thing for our family," Sue assured him.

When they arrived Friday evening, they told the other team members that's what they had come for. They were expecting a miracle. In fact, it seemed they had told everyone except Larry and Steve. They had not even mentioned the healing service to the boys because they didn't want them to have any fears or dread, not knowing what to expect. They were confident that they could move comfortably into that situation and that God would be with them.

Friday night at the opening session of the Teen Section, the leader said, "I'd like to ask each one of you to state what you believe at this point and tell us where you are in your Christian faith."

What?! Larry panicked. *I'm not ready for this! Not in front of all these strange kids and adults!*

He scrambled to his feet and bolted from the room, leaving Steve contentedly behind.

Outside the double doors, he found himself face to face with not only Don Bartow but also Bruce Larson, then national president of Faith at Work, and Heidi Frost, another national level Faith at Work leader.

"Hey, buddy, what's the problem?" Bartow asked.

"I can't hack that," he jerked his head back toward the closed doors.

"Really?" The leaders looked at each other.

Then Bruce Larson said, "Well, everyone is involved in groups somewhere. You want to hang around with us?"

"Sure," Larry said, relieved at not being sent back in.

"Okay, let's go get something to drink."

The healing service that Saturday afternoon went as Sue and Bill had anticipated. It was a quiet, spiritual, deep moment, the church at prayer. Don Bartow asked all those present to pray for each other and for those going forward for healing. He wanted them to be constantly in prayer during the entire service.

People went forward, singly or in groups of two or more. They knelt, hands were laid on heads or shoulders, and their requests were prayed for. Not only were physical healings implored, but also emotional, spiritual, and relational healings. Quietly, reassuringly, Bartow told them, "God's biggest concern is the healing of the spirit. He wants us with Him. Christ is our intercessor. He died to forgive our sins. If you feel unforgiven, if you feel that you don't have a right relationship with God, if you haven't accepted Christ as your savior, you certainly can pray for any of these things. Healing is a broad term. And God, the Great Physician, will answer your prayers."

The Pattons sat quietly for a while. This was a totally new experience for Larry and Steve. Their parents seemed at ease, eyes closed in prayer. The boys watched with great curiosity as people they had met that weekend went forward for prayers with the leaders, who were standing in a semi-circle facing the congregation.

Then suddenly, but very softly, Dad said, "C'mon, boys, let's go forward for prayer." He stepped out into the aisle and waited as Sue, then Larry, then Steve began the carpeted walk to the front of the sanctuary. Bill brought up the rear of their little procession.

They knelt together in front of Don Bartow. He laid hands on each one of them and prayed a particular prayer of healing appropriate to the one he was touching. Then they returned to their seats, tears blurring their vision. Larry cried for a long time.

There was no instantaneous healing for Larry that day. But Bill and Sue's faith was unshaken. Remembering Tom Kirkman's concern about what might happen in this circumstance, Sue felt she must reassure the other participants at the Faith At Work Conference.

Sunday there was a time of sharing. It was not a time for members of the leadership team to speak, but Sue took the microphone anyway and addressed the gathering.

"Yesterday in the healing service, Bill and I and our two sons, Larry and Steve, went forward for a prayer for instantaneous healing for Larry, who has CP. We came expecting a miracle, as many of you know. Larry was not healed instantaneously. I'm sure you're wondering where we stand now. What is our relationship with God at this point?

"We believe that God is working in our lives. We trust Him, we know He loves us, and we believe He is working out a miracle for us. Apparently Larry's healing is gradual, day to day, minute by minute. It's God's perfect timing, His perfect plan. Larry is being taken care of, just as surely as God works instantaneously in others' lives. When we prayed, we knew that whatever happened would be good."

She sat down amid applause and calls of "Praise the Lord, praise the Lord anyway!" Someone sitting behind Larry clapped him on the shoulder encouragingly.

Larry was still arguing with the Lord. He had invited Jesus to be Lord of his life. He had joined the church. He had even gone to the Faith At Work Conference in Ohio and gone forward for prayers for healing. Yet nothing had changed. He certainly hadn't been healed. And he didn't feel any different inside, either. What was the big deal? Was God there or not?

Then someone told him, "If you ask the Lord, He will be there even if you don't feel any different for a while."

"Oh. Okay." *My life is okay,* Larry thought. *No big deal.*

One night in November, 1970, Eunice Bitzer invited some members of the Youth Fellowship to her home to meet Betty

Watson. Six or seven kids showed up, Larry among them. Betty talked for some time, and then she brought up the subject of the Baptism of the Holy Spirit.

"It's not enough to believe in Christ," she told them. "You have to ask for the Baptism of the Holy Spirit. When you receive that, then God's spirit completely fills you. You are fully alive in Christ, and great things will happen."

When Betty finished, one of the young girls, Pam, asked if Betty would pray for her to receive the Holy Spirit.

"How about me, too?" Larry asked.

No one else was willing to risk it.

Betty prayed for Pam and Larry, and both did receive the Baptism of the Holy Spirit. Pam was teary-eyed, and Larry was excited, exhilarated.

When he got home that night, the house was dark. Mom and Dad were asleep, but Larry couldn't wait to share his good news. He knocked softly on their bedroom door.

Mom sat up in bed, turned on the light, and blinked at him. "What's the matter, Larry?"

"Nothing's wrong. I just wanted to tell you I received the Baptism of the Holy Spirit tonight!"

"Larry! That's wonderful! Praise the Lord! How do you feel?"

"Man! Like I'm on fire! Betty Watson talked about it, and then Pam asked her to pray for her to get it, and I said, 'Me, too!'"

"I knew Betty would be talking about that tonight," Mom admitted. "Oh Larry, I'm so happy for you!"

Larry was excited, but he didn't know just what to expect. He was "on fire for the Lord" for a long time, but nothing really changed.

In August of '71, Bill bought a camper and the family took off for a five-week tour of the West. Through a couple of chance encounters before they left home, they had learned about a charismatic conference to be held at Melodyland in Anaheim, California, and rearranged their itinerary to include that. Katherine Kuhlman, a woman with a widely known healing ministry, was to be there, and she would also hold a healing service at Shrine Auditorium in Los Angeles.

In Mrs. Kuhlman's services, she did not ask people to come forward for prayers for healing. Emphasizing that it was God, not she, who healed, she prayed for His merciful healing in general. People in the auditorium could appropriate those prayers for themselves. If they experienced healing then and there, and many did, they were invited to come forward to tell about it.

Several significant things happened for the Pattons during that week. At the Kuhlman service at the Shrine Auditorium, they heard the testimony of a young man who had been instantaneously healed of CP two months earlier.

Sitting in the audience in a complete body brace, this young man had felt as though someone had placed hands on his head and was praying for him. He felt heat go down through his whole body, he said, and he knew instantly that he had been healed. He tried to get people to remove his body brace, but, oddly enough in those circumstances, no one would. So he went on home, removed it himself, and confirmed what he already knew. His body was perfectly controlled and no longer distorted.

Naturally the Pattons were excited to hear that. They praised the Lord and expected a similar miracle for Larry during that week.

One night at the conference, both Larry and Steve went forward for prayers. Two men prayed with them. After considering Larry's obvious needs for a while, they ended by praying for Steve to accept Christ. Larry was delighted that his brother made that decision. *That's really neat,* he thought.

For Steve this was just a formal commitment of what he'd

pretty much believed anyway. And, like the rest of the family, his life didn't change a whole lot for a year or so after that.

Ralph Wilkerson, the minister of the Melodyland church where the conference was held, heard about the Pattons and their prayers for Larry's healing. He invited the four of them to his office. After a few preliminary remarks, he said to Larry and Steve, "God has wonderful plans for your lives. Do you know what that means?"

By this time Larry had come to understand a little bit more of what Christianity was all about, so he answered, "Yeah."

"Do you know what God wants you to do?"

"Yeah."

"You do, Larry?" Mom questioned.

"Not exactly, but I'm open."

Rev. Wilkerson pursued, "Are you open to being in the ministry?"

"Yeah. Whatever."

The minister concluded the interview by praying for each member of the family.

The last night of the conference, they attended their second Kuhlman service of healing. Their anticipation for Larry was intense. Mrs. Kuhlman began her prayers for God's healing power to touch people in the arena. The audience was instructed that if any one became aware of having been healed, he should come forward and report it to some of her aides who were waiting to pray with them.

The four of them sat, holding each others' hands, squeezing tightly. The bursitis in Bill's elbow hurt with that exertion, but even as he noticed it, he disregarded it. This might be the moment of Larry's healing. Bill concentrated on prayers for Larry.

Suddenly, completely unexpectedly, Bill's bursitis was healed!

"Thank you, Lord," he murmured and went on praying for

Larry.

"If you are aware of a healing taking place within you, confirm that by coming forward and reporting to one of my aides," Mrs. Kuhlman reiterated.

So, to the amazement of his family, Bill quietly excused himself and went forward, swinging his forearm freely. The rest of them continued in prayer.

I know I'm a Christian, Larry thought. *This is gonna be It!* Nothing happened.

Here I am, Lord. Come on!

He knew he hadn't been healed.

What went wrong? he wondered. *Why didn't it happen?*

He was upset and disappointed, but he did not give up. *I may be an immature Christian,* he told himself, *but I know enough not to give up on the Lord.*

"Mom, why didn't it happen to me?" he asked later that night.

"Don't be discouraged, Larry. The Lord knows what's best for you. Remember? He has a perfect plan for your life. And He has a place and a time for your healing."

12

New Vine

"Don't forget, Larry, I'm taking you to New Vine this Friday night," Paul Irwin said firmly.

"No way."

"Yes, I am. You said you'd go."

"Changed my mind."

"Oh no you don't! You're going. This Friday."

"Got other plans."

"Larry, I listened to your problems all last weekend at the Winter Retreat. Our friendship really deepened. I know it, and you do, too. And I told you then that what you really need is what New Vine has to offer. I've been telling you about this for months now. You can see how it's changed me. I'll pick you up at 6:30. You're going!"

The winter retreat had been a great experience because of his long talks with Paul, Larry remembered. So many things had been bothering him lately, really getting him down. Though he had lots of surface friends at school and church, there was no one that he could really open up to. Then somehow, at the Senior High Fellowship retreat, he had been able to unload on Paul.

Paul Irwin, Kathie and John's son, was two years older than Larry. They had grown up together in the church, and their parents were good friends. But until this weekend, Larry had not felt particularly close to Paul.

Paul had invited Larry to New Vine before; in fact, he had invited the whole Senior High Fellowship. Larry knew it was a large, non-denominational, Spirit-filled group of teens and young adults in the Detroit area who met every Friday night in a Presbyterian church seven or eight miles in toward the city. That was what put him off. Too many strangers. How would they accept him, being handicapped? It was always agonizing meeting strangers. They couldn't understand his speech until they got to know him pretty well. They often assumed he was mentally retarded and talked down to him. And people always stared. He hated it.

He had told Paul last weekend that he would go. But the closer Friday came, the more he tried to find a way out. By Friday he was nearly sick about it. But Paul picked him up at 6:30, and they went to New Vine.

The brick church with the two story classroom building was visible from the interchange of Southfield Freeway and Six Mile Drive. The parking lot was filling rapidly. Paul and Larry made their way from the car to the double-sized blue classroom amid friendly greetings and introductions. *Not too bad so far,* Larry thought.

At 7:15 the service of song, prayer, and praise began. Larry could sense a love and joy in the people there. Their songs rang out, filling the room. Some gave testimonies, and some prayed. Some spoke in languages Larry had never heard. "Is that 'speaking in tongues'?" he whispered to Paul. Paul nodded, his face aglow.

Time flew. It seemed impossible that it was 9:00. Then the leader announced that it was time to go to class from 9:30 to 10:30. These seven- or eight-week classes ran all the time, on topics like "Foundations," "Life in the Spirit," "Bible Study," or "The Jesus Talk." There was a one-time-only class, "Explanation," for those attending New Vine for the first time. By the end of the song and praise service, Larry felt comfortable enough to attend the "Explanation" class on his own. Paul went to his Bible study class.

In the Explanation class, new people were divided into two groups according to whether they had yet committed their lives to Christ. In Larry's group there was a question and answer session about their religious experience and what New Vine had to offer. That hour, too, was over all too quickly.

"Paul, thanks for dragging me down here tonight," Larry said as they started home. "That was fantastic!"

"You didn't make it easy!" Paul laughed. "But I knew you'd love it. What about next week?"

"Wouldn't miss it!"

As soon as a new class began, Larry enrolled in the Life in the Spirit seminar, led by Dave Horning and others. During the fifth week of the seven-week series, the leaders laid hands on members and prayed, either for the Baptism of the Holy Spirit or, if that had already been given, for some other need. This fifth session was the high point of the seminar. During the preceding week, the leaders phoned each member to see if he were ready for the laying on of hands.

When Dave called Larry with this question, Larry calmly replied, "Yep."

Dave was surprised that Larry was so much at peace about it. Most class members were quite nervous, even apprehensive. "How do you want us to pray for you, Larry?"

"I've already received the Baptism of the Holy Spirit," Larry told him, "so would you lay hands on me for a healing of my body?"

"You've got it, buddy," Dave agreed. "I want you to know that all of us leaders will be fasting all day Friday in preparation for this. We always do before this fifth session."

That Friday evening, New Vine began with the song and praise service as usual. Although only 25 or 30 were enrolled in the Life in the Spirit seminar, all 250 or 300 people there were aware that this was the night for the laying on of hands in that class. There was a special fervor, an intense anticipation in the whole crowd.

Larry thought, *I'm 16 years old, and I've already been to two or three healing services led by some real bigwigs. Wouldn't it be great for my healing to come through this group of kids?!*

In the seminar that night, several people received the Baptism of the Holy Spirit. Larry was the last one to be prayed for. The word had spread that they would pray for his physcial healing.

When it was his turn, Larry sat in the middle of the floor, legs extended straight out, back straight, without moving. It was a position he had never managed before.

Everyone clustered around, and six or seven laid hands on him. For over an hour he sat, without moving, while prayers of rejoicing and songs of praise literally filled the air without ceasing. The atmosphere was electric.

Members of other groups, whose classes had ended at the regular time, crowded outside the door trying to see in the little window. They could sense the presence of the Holy Spirit in there, but all they could see was a tightly formed circle around someone sitting on the floor.

As the prayers ascended on his behalf, Larry kept his eyes tightly closed. *This is so great,* he thought. *I know now is the right time for the Lord to heal me. I just feel the Lord here with us.*

Then, very close to his ear, he heard one of the leaders say, "Larry, it's going to be a gradual thing. It's not going to happen all at once."

When he finally opened his eyes, Larry could not believe an hour had gone by. Dave said, "Larry, you've sat like that for an hour!"

"No, I couldn't have."

"But you did! Praise the Lord!"

They helped him to his feet. Everyone there seemed to tingle from the whole experience. They walked Larry to the car, still exclaiming and praising God.

Next morning, after a very sound sleep, Larry suddenly realized he was awake even before he opened his eyes. Instantly he recalled all the details of the previous night.

How will I know if I'm healed? he wondered, lying very still. *It will take me a few weeks to learn how to write smoothly.*

With a sudden idea, he threw back the covers, pulled on jeans and shoes and socks, and went out in the yard to run as fast as he could.

Well, that hasn't changed.

It never occurred to him to look in a mirror. He didn't avoid mirrors—he just never thought to look in one.

The healing, apparently, *was* to be a gradual one. From then on, each new accomplishment, even minute progress, was taken by the New Vine members as proof that God truly was healing Larry.

But still Larry longed for a miraculous, instantaneous healing. When Katherine Kuhlman came to Detroit, the whole family went to the healing service in Ford Auditorium. Again, others were healed, but not Larry. Mrs. Kuhlman went to Ann Arbor. So did the Pattons.

By this time, though, Larry had matured in his faith. He hoped for the final completion of the gradual healing, but if it didn't happen, then life would go on.

At school, Mrs. Ludwig, a counselor, became aware of all this pursuit of a miracle and questioned Sue about it. "I certainly hope you're not going to let Larry just sit and do nothing until God performs this miracle!"

"Oh, no!" Sue assured her, shocked at the very idea. "We believe medical science is a gift from God that He expects us to use. Prayer and medicine and therapy should be used together. We've never quit taking Larry to the doctor or to therapy. We thank God for providing these kind and loving people who work so patiently with him."

The whole family attended the CFO camp that summer, and there, too, Larry asked someone to lay hands on him and pray for healing. Again, nothing seemed to happen.

Many well-meaning Christians told them if they had enough faith, God would heal Larry. "Someone in your family is a cynic, or God is trying to teach one of you a lesson about something. You are doing something to prevent this healing."

But from their study of the scriptures, all four of them rejected these Job's comforters. The Pattons had learned that God is not boxed in by formulas. He operates by His perfect plan for each one of them. He will not withhold His gifts from those who trust Him and seek His will.

And then Sue's German practicality reasserted itself. "Look," she told her family, "God can heal Larry anytime, anywhere He wants to. We've prayed about it; we've turned it over to the Lord. That's enough. We don't need to drag ourselves all over the country for these healing services."

In September, 1972, Don Bartow led another Faith At Work Conference at the Redford Baptist Church. Several of Pattons' friends testified about how the Lord was working in their lives. Jim Langdal spoke briefly about New Vine and the spiritual growth that he had experienced there. Then Don called on Larry Patton to say a few words.

Larry knew that many people in the audience had attended the Findlay conference two years earlier when he and Steve and Mom and Dad had first prayed for his healing. He felt that the Lord was speaking through him as he told everyone how discouraged he had been about healing. Then he told them about the laying on of hands at New Vine and his new trust that the Lord was healing him gradually.

The audience was moved by his words, but the Pattons and

a few others who knew him well were awestruck. For the first time ever, Larry's speech was clear. Every syllable was distinct and smooth. The miracle lasted only as long as it took for Larry to give his testimony. After that, his speech returned to what for him was normal. Larry himself was unaware that his speech sounded different to others. He was aware only that the Lord was speaking through him.

A year later, the Pattons attended another Faith At Work Conference led by Bartow, this time in Columbus, Ohio. Again Larry was asked to testify. This time his audience struggled to understand him. His words revealed a depth of understanding and growth in the Christian faith.

"I've kind of turned my mind away from my healing because I realized I've been thinking more about my healing than about the Lord. So I've put that on the back burner."

He went on to speak about insights he'd acquired and ventures in faith through the New Vine community. Then he concluded, "The Lord is going to heal me, whether in this life or the next. We all know that in eternity I'm going to have the same whole body that you have. We'll all be equal, whatever our bodies are. So for now, I'm going to focus my attention on the Lord, and the healing comes when it comes."

13

A Relatively Normal Adolescence

"Why are we stopping here, Dad?" Larry asked as Bill pulled the car out of the morning rush hour traffic and into a deserted parking lot. Bill was driving Larry to school.

"Because you're going to drive the rest of the way," Bill answered.

"No way! You gotta be kidding! I can't drive in all this traffic."

"I guess we'll just sit here, then, until the rush is over."

They sat there in silence for a few minutes. Then Larry pleaded, "I have a history test first period, Dad. We'd better get goin'."

"Whenever you're ready to drive," Bill replied calmly.

"But this is Woodward Avenue. Look at that traffic!" Larry was shaking all over.

Practicing in the Driver's Ed car was one thing. Driving the family car down quiet streets in the neighborhood wasn't bad either. Larry had done well in Driver's Ed, and Dad had given him lots of extra hours practice with the Driver's Ed car he used for high school classes. But this was morning rush hour on Woodward Avenue!

He stole a look at Dad. He was placidly reading the morning paper. Larry could tell he would actually sit there until they were both late for school. Immovable. Like a mountain!

Larry watched the traffic whiz by. Drivers changed lanes,

impatiently blasting their horns. Trucks ground into lower gears, diesel smoke blackening the air. Traffic lights changed from green to yellow to red and brakes screamed. He tried to imagine himself coping with that mad race. The thought was terrifying. He glanced again at Old Man Mountain sitting next to him.

Then a verse from last night's Bible study at New Vine came to his mind: "If ye have faith and doubt not, ye shall not only do this . . . but also if ye shall say unto this mountain, be thou removed . . . it shall be done. And all things, whatsoever ye shall ask in prayer, believing, ye shall receive." (Matthew 21:21-22)

Well, Lord, he gulped silently, *You better help me with this. Dad's really gonna make me do it, so please get me to school safely. Please be in the driver's seat with me.* "Okay, Dad. Switch places. I'll try it."

Concentrating as hard as he ever had for the "Doctor's Walk," Larry guided the car safely to Kimball High. He pulled into the parking lot grinning triumphantly. *We did it, Lord!* he exulted silently.

"Good job!" Bill said. "I wouldn't have made you do it if I hadn't known you could. And I also knew that you'd never try it unless I made you. I think you're ready now to take the test for your license."

After driving in rush hour traffic, Larry confidently passed the written and road tests for a Michigan Operator's License. However, the examiners were doubtful about issuing an unrestricted license to someone as obviously handicapped as he. They asked for a written statement from a doctor saying that he should be allowed to drive with no restrictions. Dr. LaMont of the D.O.C. was happy to oblige.

So by the time he was a high school senior, Larry could drive Steve and some friends into Detroit on Friday nights for New Vine. He and Flip Hoffman could cruise around after

Senior High Fellowship on Wednesday nights, chasing each other and playing hide-and-seek on side streets in a hilly section of Huntington Woods, near the church. He could pick up Peter for a Junior Deacon's meeting. And he could drive to practices and games to work as student manager for the Kimball High School basketball team.

Bill had spent the whole summer of 1972 remodeling the basement. The enormous furnace with its rotund metal body and fat, far-reaching ducts had squatted like an obese monster in a cave, consuming space. When it had been dismembered and carted out, with the help of some New Vine kids who happened to be upstairs at the right time, Bill finished the basement with light wood paneling and bright lights. It became a spacious game room for the boys and their friends. There was always a case of pop and a stereo to add to the cheer.

The Patton home was the center of activity for Larry, Steve, and their friends. There were seven of them altogether, all members of First Presbyterian Church but representing three different high schools. In decent weather they played basketball in the driveway. In winter, it was pingpong in the basement.

Steve was by far the best player. The boys had continuous tournaments, and Steve was always the one the others most wanted to beat. A couple of times Larry managed to do that. Beating his brother, the champion, was especially sweet.

It was a busy, happy, fulfilling life. His personality was cheerful and highly competitive. Larry was a hard worker. He had to work hard to keep his grades up. Mom and Dad insisted on that if he wanted to do all those extra things.

Just doing regular assignments took more effort for him than for his classmates because he had to type everything, using only his right forefinger. Aides wrote out math problems as he dictated them. Because of the CP, his eyes had trouble "tracking" words on a page, so reading was very difficult. Therefore, all his reading assignments were tape-recorded for him, and then he listened as he tried to follow along on the page.

In junior high, he had taped all class lectures and then Mom transcribed them for him to study in the same manner: listening and following on the printed page. In high school, Larry took carbon paper to class, found a bright student, and asked him to make a copy of his notes. This saved Mom a lot of time. While his classmates took written tests, an aide took Larry and a copy of the test to the Resource Room for Handicapped Students where he typed his answers to the questions or dictated them to an aide.

He took a full academic load, following the college preparatory curriculum, and he maintained a B average. No wonder he was nominated for membership in the National Honor Society. But even more thrilling to Larry was the varsity letter he earned as student manager of the basketball team.

14

Preparing for an Independent Future

"Mrs. Patton? This is Mrs. Ludwig, the Special Ed. counselor at Kimball High," the voice on the phone said. "Now that Larry is a junior in high school, we need to be making some plans for his future."

"Yes, we've already been thinking about that."

"I'm sure you have. We do want him to be as independent as possible, don't we. It's time for you to make an appointment for him with Miriam King, the Rehabilitation Consultant for the Oakland County Schools Vocational Rehabilitation Services. The Voc Rehab will evaluate Larry and develop an appropriate plan for helping him select a potential vocational field. Then they will help him through the necessary training and job placement."

"Larry already has a pretty good idea of what he wants to do."

"I believe he mentioned something about computers when I talked to him last week?"

"Yes, that's right."

"Well, make an appointment with Miriam King and let's get started on this. Her phone number is 338-1011."

"Okay. Thanks a lot, Mrs. Ludwig."

So this is the next step, Sue thought. Ever since Larry's CP had first been diagnosed when he was two years old, they had put themselves trustingly in the hands of experts, first the D.O.C. and the Oakland County Schools Special Ed. personnel. The Pattons had faithfully done exactly what they were told. Becase Bill and Sue were teachers, they respected the professional competence of the Special Ed. people. The Pattons were not trained in that field, so they didn't try to second guess or question decisions.

They had attended annual staffing conferences at D.O.C. and at school, intimidating meetings where all the experts sat around a table and evaluated Larry's progress and made recommendations for the next year. Do this; do that. You can stop that exercise; begin this one. Larry should attend D.O.C. nursery school. Larry is ready for Tyler Orthopedic Unit now at age four and a half. Larry should attend sixth grade at Emerson, not Tyler, then go on to Adams Junior High. Kimball High School had the Special Ed. facilities Larry needs. A Servicar will provide transportation.

Only once had they asserted themselves. At the staffing conference when Larry was in sixth grade they heard for the third year in a row that he had "a reading problem." Finally Sue spoke up: "What are you going to do about his reading problem? You've been saying this for three years now, but as far as I can see, nothing is being done about it."

Twelve or fifteen pairs of eyes stared at her, silenced temporarily by her challenge. Then Mrs. Chapin, the case worker from D.O.C., said rather patronizingly, "We're working on it, Mrs. Patton. Don't be such a worrier. We know what we're doing. You don't have to push." To the others present, she said, "Mrs. Patton is very aggressive."

Sue's temper flared. "All of you work with Larry and go home at night. I am his mother, and when he is twenty years old if he can't do everything possible according to his ability or potential, I will have to feel guilty and live with it. You won't."

No one looked directly at her. The therapists played with

their pencils. The teachers doodled on the corners of the pages before them. Then the coordinator of Special Ed. cleared his throat and asked the reading specialist for a recommendation.

"It might help if someone taped all Larry's reading assignments and he could listen and follow along in the book."

Bill and Sue looked at each other. They knew who that "someone" would be. It would be a tremendous amount of time and work. But these people were the experts, the ones who could tell them what to do to help Larry achieve his full potential. "Fine. We'll do it that way," Bill assented.

It had been a lot of work, very time consuming. They found help from the Michigan Library for the Blind and Physically Handicapped and other organizations that taped material for the blind. But whatever it took, it was worth it for Larry to be an independent, self-sufficient adult. They did not want him to be a burden to them and certainly not to Steve.

Now five years later, they were being handed on to the next agency, the Michigan Department of Vocational Rehabilitation Services, which had an office in every county and a direct liaison with the county school districts.

Larry met with Miriam King on April 11, 1973, for a preliminary interview for Voc Rehab. On the form she filled out, she listed under "Service Needs and Order of Priority": General medical exam; Psychological evaluation; Reading evaluation; Speech evaluation; Reports to VRS counselor for guidance re: appropriate vocational goals.

[From this point on, lengthy quotations will be used from the Michigan Department of Education Vocational Rehabilitation Services Counselors Case Reports. Larry obtained photocopies of these pages for background material for this book. All quotations used, though edited, are exactly as found on the VRS records.]

COUNSELORS CASE REPORT:

6-19-73 CLIENT SEEN

Client and his father were seen for an office appointment this date. Client is currently 17, and will be a senior at Kimball next year. Client has his driver's license and transportation is available.

Client has an appointment to have his general medical completed on June 22nd. His performance in school has been quite good, and he has approximately a 3.4 G.P.A. Client is currently working cutting lawns 5 to 6 days a week from 3:30 to 6 p.m., earning $2 an hour. He lives near Greenfield and 12 Mile, and most of his friends come from Berkley High School. Transportation is provided to Kimball by Servicar. Client's speech is somewhat of a problem, but generally understandable. Client was quite spastic due to his cerebral palsy involvement, however, it appears that he frequently forgets to take his medication. Client has a perceptual problem with reading, and utilizes tapes, records or readers for his school work. It seems that math is his best subject, and he is interested in obtaining training in the computer field. Client uses an electric typewriter, and types one handed. Client had a chance to attend the summer program at SEOVEC in Data Processing, but due to his job cutting lawns and his desire to "goof off and have some free time," he decided not to attend. In this respect, Mrs. Ludwig, client's teacher-counselor, also reports that this summer program emphasizes computer operation, and not programming, and this is another reason why he decided not to attend. Client does lapidary work as a hobby, and makes quite a bit of jewelry. He would like his work evaluated by the craft coordinator for possible sale, however, has not made much jewelry lately, and therefore the craft coordinator will be contacted later in July to evaluate his work. On a reading evaluation done by Mrs. Rubin at Kimball, client achieved at the 8.8 reading level. Client is supposed to get a tutor to help him with reading this summer, and his parents will be arranging this. His father mentioned that Mrs. Rubin is planning to work with him this summer to increase his reading skills next year at Kimball. It was felt by this counselor, and suggested by Miriam King in her report, that an evaluation at DLH [Detroit League for the Handicapped] may be useful in further ascertaining client's physical capabilities. It also appears that client does not wish to become involved in an evaluation at the League this summer due to the fact that this would interfere with his lawn cutting and his free time. Also, Mrs. Ludwig seriously questions the usefulness of this evaluation, and therefore, client will not be referred to the League for an evaluation at this time. Mrs. Ludwig has contacted Mr. Norman Henry who works for IBM, and she has arranged an appointment to have client visit Mr. Henry at IBM for a visit and evaluation . . .

"What did you think of that, Larry?" Bill questioned him as they pulled out of the small parking lot.

Larry shrugged. "Didn't seem like a very helpful place. And more tests! Why is it every time we go some place new, they want more tests? Why can't they use the tests I've already had?"

"I guess they want the latest results. What did you think of the counselor?"

"At first he seemed friendly, but then . . . He doesn't think I can work with computers, but already I know more about math and computers than he does."

"You had the answer figured out for that math problem he gave you before he had the *problem* figured out, didn't you."

"Yeah. I don't want to take much time with this Voc Rehab this summer. I've got eight lawns to do now, and I want to enjoy the summer vacation before my senior year."

"Well, it will be interesting to meet with Mr. Henry at IBM. It was nice of Mrs. Ludwig and Mrs. Giffin to set that up for you."

"Yeah. Mrs. Giffin's husband works with Mr. Henry for IBM. Did you know that?"

"So the two counselors, Mrs. Giffin and Mrs. Ludwig, put their heads together, huh?"

"Yeah. That's gonna be neat to go to IBM and talk to him."

The meeting with Mr. Henry took place at the old Data Center of IBM in Southfield. The steel and glass room was filled with computers, cold, impersonal. It was overwhelming to Sue and quite impressive to Larry as they went in with Mrs. Ludwig and Mrs. Giffin.

Mr. Henry, in contrast to his surroundings, was warm and friendly. He introduced them to another executive and to two young employees, recent college graduates. These two young men demonstrated computers to Larry, and everyone in the group discussed IBM as a company and computers as a career choice.

"We have one employee who has cerebral palsy. In fact, he's much more severely affected than you, Larry. He's homebound," Mr. Henry said. "We've placed a terminal in his home, and he's doing good work for us."

If that guy can do it, I'm sure I can. Larry told himself. *I think that's what Mr. Henry is implying, too.*

"What should I do, then?" he asked. "Do I need a two-year degree, or four, or just start to work after high school?"

"Get a four year degree," Mr. Henry replied firmly. "This is a growing field, and you need good preparation, so go to college for a four year degree."

Larry decided right then. Any company that made machines like this, that placed a terminal in the house of a homebound employee, that was a leader in a growing field—why, that was exactly the company he'd like to work for. If it took four years of college, fine. He'd get four years of college. Whatever it took!

The two younger men showed him some programs on one of the computers and let him use the terminal. It was great fun for Larry, and it demonstrated to Mr. Henry and everyone else that he was physically and intellectually capable of handling a computer.

COUNSELORS CASE REPORT

7-16-73 CASE INFORMATION

Mrs. Ludwig contacted this counselor with respect to client's visit to IBM. Mr. Henry from IBM felt that client could physically do the work, however, they were somewhat concerned about his ability to handle the smaller cards. Mrs. Ludwig plans to administer some testing to client with respect to computer aptitude areas, and further planning will follow in September.

The required psychological testing for Voc Rehab took place on August 8, 1973. Richard Brozovich, Ph. D., the Educational

Psychologist who administered the test for Oakland County Schools, wrote in the Summary and Recommendations section of the report:

> Larry is a young man with moderate physical involvement from cerebral palsy. He is ambulatory and has been able to maintain approximately a "B" average on a high school curriculum. Intellectual evaluation indicates verbal ability at the high end of the average range. Teacher and counselor comments along with past records indicate a high degree of motivation and perseverance toward achievement. Academic deficits are apparent in the areas of reading and spelling, and Larry is currently involved in tutorial efforts to improve in these areas. Good academic skills are present in the area of mathematics.

> Larry appears to be a reasonable candidate for eventual enrollment in college based on his demonstrated motivation and persistence and the presence of sufficient verbal intelligence to complete a college curriculum in the future. In selecting a potential vocational field, close attention must be given to Larry's physical disabilities and the presence of minimal reading skills. Larry's proven ability in the area of mathematics seems to provide the area of greatest promise for future preparation and eventual employment. Suggested fields in the past such as computer programming, bookkeeping, or other mathematical skill areas seem to be practical alternatives.

> Eventual selection of an occupational field must take into account his poor speech quality and his inability to write or print with even minimal

speed and accuracy.

But the VRS report shows none of these positive comments.

COUNSELORS CASE REPORT

9-12-73 CASE INFORMATION

Client's psychological testing has been received from Oakland Schools. Due to his cerebral palsy, client is unable to write legibly, has a speech impairment, and poor motor coordination. On the WRAT from 1972, he obtained a reading level at the 5th grade and math at the 12th. During the Oakland Schools testing it took a great deal of effort for him to even approximate printing his first name. On the WAIS he obtained a Verbal IQ of 108. Client is currently involved in tutorial sessions with respect to his reading and spelling difficulties. The selection of his occupational field must take into account his poor speech and inability to write or print.

11-2-73 CLIENT SEEN

Client and his mother were seen for an office appointment this date. Client's mother definitely wants him to go on for further training after high school . . .

In talking with the client alone he informed this counselor that he is not at all sure about college attendance or further training. He did indicate the possibility of obtaining a job without further training after graduation in stock work or in a lapidary shop. He states that after two or three pages, he loses his concentration. Client is quite

limited due to his disability with respect to any
activities which involve manual dexterity, reading
or writing. Based upon the information currently
available, it is this counselor's opinion that a four
year college program is not realistic. With respect
to computer programming, Mrs. Ludwig stated that
the personnel at IBM informed her that all the work
is performed on a typewriter, however, this
counselor has visited the director of Control Data
Institute, and he stated that most of a programmer's
work is handwritten charts and flow charts, and
good handwriting ability is necessary.

"That was awful!" Sue sputtered as they left the cramped
office of the Voc Rehab. "His manner was so . . ." she
searched for just the right word, ". . . *demeaning!* He thinks
I'm domineering and aggressive because I don't think the
Detroit League for the Handicapped needs to evaluate your
work! You don't want to make rock jewelry for a living! You
want professional training. DLH can't evaluate that!"

She stopped for a minute, pushed her glasses back up, and
then, looking suspiciously at Larry, she asked, "What did
you talk about all that time I was sitting out in the waiting
room?"

"I told him I'm not sure I want to go to college this fall."

"You *what*?! Why on earth did you say that, Larry?"

"Mom, I've been going to school all my life! I'm tired of
it. I'm tired of trying to find people to take notes for me and
write my tests for me. I'm tired of listening to tapes and following along in the book. Up to this point I've had no choice.
But I don't have to go to college."

But I really do, he told himself. *With two parents with
masters' degrees, I know deep down I'm going to college.*

Then Mom surprised him. She took him quite seriously

and answered calmly, "I bet you do feel that way, Larry. I probably would, too."

Once before she had responded that way. He was in seventh grade at Adams Junior High and the principal had called him in to congratulate him. "Larry, you've been elected treasurer of the Student Council. Congratulations. All the Detroit area student council officers will be going to Eastern Michigan University for a training conference the day of . . ."

Larry had burst into tears and had cried hysterically. Fortunately, his mother was coming to pick him up to go to Emerson School for therapy at that time, so the principal had turned the sobbing boy over to her with only a hurried explanation.

On the way to Emerson Larry managed to say through his tears, "I don't want to go to EMU for a day. I'm scared!"

Mom thought for a minute and then said, "Well, Larry, I don't blame you. I think at your age I'd have been scared, too. Don't worry about it."

He had instantly felt better, and he did this time, too. She understood. That took off a world of pressure.

So, with the pressure removed, Larry began to make plans to attend Wayne State University in Detroit. Not only did they have a good course of study in mathematics and computer science, but also they were equipped to service handicapped students. It was not a residential campus. Larry would live at home and commute to class.

Betsy Ferris was in charge of the resource center for handicapped students at Wayne State. Her office provided tape recorders, a place to study or to take tests, and whatever additional help her clients needed. There were scores of handicapped students at WSU, and Betsy knew them well. She was a good person to consult about Larry's chances for success in a university setting. Sue and Larry met with her for an hour and a half.

COUNSELORS CASE REPORT

12-17-73 CASE INFORMATION

Call was received from Betsy Ferris at Wayne State University. She feels that client can handle college work with assistance, i.e. readers, tape recorders, etc., however, she would like to determine what the nature of his reading problem is before further planning.

12-18-73 CASE INFORMATION

Conversation was had with client's mother this date. Client is seeing Dr. Ambinder (Midwest Educational Resources Clinic) this date, and Dr. Ambinder was contacted by this counselor and he will inform this counselor as to the details of the length and cost of the perceptual evaluation shortly. Also at this time a work evaluation was discussed with client's mother. She informed this counselor that Larry does not wish to stay in Ann Arbor over Easter, but she feels he might agree to commute. It is this counselor's feeling that it would be much easier for client to remain in Ann Arbor, and he is not being realistic with respect to cooperating and obtaining the necessary vocational evaluations. As an example of this his mother stated that he didn't want to have an appointment with Dr. Ambinder any time over his Christmas vacation.

The Pattons had seen Norm Henry at IBM, and his optimistic prognosis had been conveyed to VRS. The Pattons had seen Betsy Ferris and her optimistic prognosis had been conveyed to VRS. The Pattons were following through on Ms.

Ferris's suggestion to take Larry to Dr. Ambinder's Reading Clinic.

In spite of all this, when VRS prepared the "Certification for Eligibility" document on December 19, 1973, the case worker concluded with this paragraph:

> v. NARRATIVE DOCUMENTATION
> PLAN DEVELOPMENT NARRATIVE
>
> Before a realistic vocational plan can be formulated, a number of evaluations are necessary. These will include an opthamological exam, a perceptual evaluation, and it is planned to obtain a work evaluation from MSDO at the University of Michigan. Client is currently considering college, and he was referred to Betsy Ferris at Wayne State University who feels he has the ability for success in college. However, this counselor has some questions as to the feasibility of a college program and placement in a professional area considering the client's lack of writing ability and his speech problems as well as his other limitations. Once these planned evaluations are completed, a decision will be made with respect to a vocational plan.

Larry and his parents were becoming more frustrated and disgusted with VRS with every contact. The purpose of the agency was to develop a realistic vocational plan and provide the help needed to realize it. Larry had already developed his own plan, and every resource person he consulted confirmed that it was realistic to assume that he could do well in computers. But VRS couldn't seem to accept that. Were they upset because Larry had developed his goals without their help? Did they have only Plan A, Plan B, Plan C, or

Plan D, and Larry didn't fit any of their pre-arranged plans?

"Who needs 'em?" Bill roared. "Every time we go over there, they challenge everything Larry says and then try to belittle him! Tell your mother what the caseworker said today, Larry."

"He asked me why I thought I could handle college level math classes. I told him I was getting a B in senior math at Kimball, and he said, 'Senior math? That's the simplest math course offered to seniors, isn't it?' I said, 'No! It's calculus!'"

"See?" Bill insisted. "Who needs 'em? We can get Larry through college without that kind of help!"

Sue tried to suppress a smile. She was amused to see that Bill was more upset than she had been after her last trip to VRS with Larry. Not that she thought there was anything amusing about what Larry had told her just now! But Bill and the boys were always saying she over-reacted. If Bill was this angry, then she hadn't over-reacted before.

"Well," she said earnestly, "we certainly will need their financial help. After next year both boys will be in college for three years—we'll need all the help we can get! Besides, this Dr. Ambinder thinks he really can help Larry improve his reading, and that's going to cost a small fortune."

At supper several days later, Sue announced, "I called Voc Rehab today about Dr. Ambinder's clinic. I don't know whether they'll help with the cost or not. And the man at Voc Rehab kept insisting on more tests! I told him Larry has had all kinds of tests already, and all those results are available to him, but he wants more."

"What kind of tests?" Bill asked.

"I asked him, and he wouldn't tell me! He just repeated that they wanted Larry to go to Ann Arbor to the University Hospital for two weeks of testing."

"No way!" Larry put in. "I can't possibly miss two weeks of school. I'd never catch up."

"Yeah, Larry, I told him that," Sue affirmed, "and then he suggested going during Spring Break and missing one week of school following the Break."

"But that's when the Junior Deacons and Deaconesses are going to McCormick Seminary in Chicago for the work trip. You know, Dad. You said you'd go, too. No way am I gonna miss that!"

"No, we're already committed to that," Bill replied. "It's not fair to ask you to give that up. Don't worry about that. But back to the reading clinic. What did he say about that?"

"He said Voc Rehab couldn't become involved in something that long-term and expensive. Then he suggested Ferndale Adult Education and Marygrove and Wayne have reading programs based on ability to pay."

"Well, check them out," Bill told her, "but be sure they can accomplish what Dr. Ambinder can."

"The VRS is just sitting on Dr. Ambinder's recommendation," Sue complained in February. "He said Larry would need help three times a week continuously through his whole college career, and the sooner he starts, the better. That was two months ago. I've checked out all these other places Voc Rehab suggested, and none of them can help Larry the way Dr. Ambinder can. I called Voc Rehab to tell them that, and nothing happened!"

"Maybe it's time to go over the caseworker's head and call his supervisor," Bill suggested.

COUNSELORS CASE REPORT

2-19-74 SUPERVISORY REVIEW

This case was called to this supervisor's attention by the counselor and by a phone call from

Mrs. Patton regarding a request for reading therapy through Dr. Ambinder. It was agreed that reading therapy might be appropriate but that it would need to be a part of a diagnostic package which would enable the counselor to make an appropriate decision regarding long-term vocational planning. It was suggested to Mrs. Patton that there was a need for current comprehensive psychological evaluation as well as precise information regarding the perceptual-organic deficits that have accompanied the cerebral palsy. Additionally, it was suggested that an evaluation such as at the University Hospital would offer more specific information regarding client's ability to function in a university setting. It might additionally assist in providing answers regarding long-term vocational goals. It was noted that Mrs. Patton was initially negative regarding further exploration, testing or evaluation but has since agreed to current evaluations in psychology, occupational therapy and speech therapy to be completed at the Detroit Orthopaedic Clinic where client is known. Mrs. Patton is agreeable to further evaluation at University Hospital if it appears necessary, to be completed some time this spring or summer. Additionally, it was agreed that the Cerebral Palsy Association would be asked to consult with this agency and with Mrs. Chapin of the Orthopaedic Clinic to assist in planning a comprehensive plan for this client. A report and recommendation has been received from Dr. Ambinder recommending early remedial therapy for this client. A suggestion is made that the reading deficit, which is presently measured at the fifth grade level in both speed and comprehension, might be substantially improved. If client's reading levels can be improved, additional vocational options may open up and it is therefore the position of this agency that reading therapy shall be provided to determine if client's reading level can be improved and if it will further raise the reading and comprehension levels so that additional vocational opportunities become available. This service will be considered a diagnostic service necessary prior to the arrival of a vocational objective or vocational plan. Initial authorization will be written to begin February 25 through June 28 at three sessions per week. The parents have made specific investigation and expect that a private insurance policy will cover some of the cost beginning late in the summer if it appears advisable to continue with the therapy at the time.

So Larry began working on his "reading problem" at Dr. Ambinder's clinic, the Educational Resources Center. Larry could tell that it would be helpful. However, it was the spring term of his senior year in high school, and many things were more important to him than the reading clinic or Voc Rehab.

One night at New Vine, Larry confided in Jim Langdal, his growth group leader. "Jim, I gotta talk to you about something personal."

"Yeah, Larry? What is it?"

"I would really like to go to the Senior Prom, but I don't have anybody to take. Plus, with my handicap I'm not to the point of feeling comfortable about asking girls to go out."

Jim nodded understandingly. "I know some of the girls in the Community [New Vine] are looking for dates to take them to proms. Let me look into setting something up for you."

A couple of weeks later, Larry received this note:

> Larry,
>
> I talked to Janice last night, but when I got back from school so many things happened I didn't get a chance to call you.
>
> Janice said that she felt peaceful about going to the Prom with you. Her parents also said yes. I told her you would call her in the next day or so and arrange to talk to her sometime. So you're all set.
>
> Jim

Larry was all set, except that he didn't even know who Janice was. All he could remember was that he had met her sometime before at a meeting.

He did call her, and they met on Sunday before the prom. Janice was a small girl, round and soft, whose sweet face glowed with Christian joy. She and Larry started and finished that first date with prayer. It was the beginning of a very special brother-sister relationship with Christ at the center.

June, 1974, was a very exciting time for Larry, with meeting Janice, going to the prom, and then graduating from high school. One of his graduation gifts was this letter from Jeff Vahlbusch, a friend from Senior High Fellowship:

> Larry,
>
> You made it! To use that old time-worn phrase, CONGRATULATIONS! The beautiful part about your graduation especially is that you have relied on Christ to bring you where you stand now and that is wonderful!
>
> Never lose the springy joy which you possess through Him—it's the only thing that stays

constant. Thank you for all that you have done for me—let's keep our love for each other strong. The Lord's really working through you, Larry, and I praise Him for that. I can't think of you without thanking our Lord.

> Love through Christ,
> Jeff Vahlbusch

P.S. Congratulations to your whole wonderful family, too!

A few weeks before graduation, Larry started looking for a summer job. He didn't think he wanted to mow lawns again. A friend told him that the Berkley Parks and Recreation Board was taking applications, so Larry applied there to work on the grounds crew. He was so confident he would be hired that he didn't even apply elsewhere.

Six weeks later he received a phone call to come in for an interview, his first ever. Nervous but still confident, he interviewed with Mr. Tooley. Finally Mr. Tooley concluded by saying, "You can start at $2.75 an hour. Is that okay?"

"Yes!" Larry exclaimed, dollar signs dancing in his eyes. No one had ever paid him that much before.

Larry wrote in his journal:

> This was just another step in God's plan for my life. In each step along the path, God has a reason or a purpose.
>
> Some people might say, "How can working for Parks and Rec serve any purpose in God's plan as far as growing deeper in His love and faith?" Over the course of four summers that helped me grow spiritually as well as growing up in life in general . . . I learned how to work and get along

with fellow workers. That was not always too easy.

Having a job where thinking was not always needed gave me time to think and pray. It was more than just working while praying to my Lord. It was like God was sitting right there talking to me while I was working.

15

College Days

That fall when Larry enrolled at Wayne State University in Detroit, he needed all the strength his faith could give. He had entered high school with no fear, but he was petrified to start college!

He felt very much alone that first day. He realized for the first time how dependent on other people he actually was. All his life Mom and Dad had told him he had to become independent and do things for himself. They refused to help him. They sized up the outer boundaries of his capabilities and made him struggle to reach them. Then they redefined "outer boundaries" and the struggle went on. But they always cheered him on, praising every accomplishment as a step toward the golden goal of becoming independent.

People at Kimball, at church, at Scouts, and at New Vine had been in the booster section, too, especially at New Vine, where each new level of accomplishment was seen as proof of gradual healing. Larry had always had a fan club supporting his efforts, even though a lot of the credit had rightfully gone to his parents and to the Lord. In his small world, he was a big star. Then he enrolled at Wayne State.

Not wanting to be late, he got to the campus early that day. He didn't know what to do with himself. At Kimball he would have gone to the Health Room, a place for handicapped students to relax and get help. The WSU equivalent was the

Educational Rehabilitation Services, where he had met Betsy Ferris a few months earlier. So Larry went there, expecting to be welcomed and told what to do.

Unlike the Health Room at Kimball, the ERS room struck Larry as cold, impersonal. No one welcomed him, and no one told him what to do. The room itself seemed to say, "Welcome to college where you are a number." He felt completely on his own. No one was going to do anything for him.

Later, in the registration line, he tried to enroll in the 16 hours of classes he had selected.

"Sorry," said the registrar. "You can take only eight hours this first term."

"What?! Who says?" Larry was shocked.

"There's a little card attached to your enrollment card that says only eight hours. I guess to see how you'll do before you try a full load."

Dismayed, Larry looked through the thick booklet of classes offered for the fall quarter. "Okay, I'll take Math 210 and . . ."

"Math 210 is already filled. What's your next choice?"

Larry ended up enrolled in a geography class and English—hardly what he had come to college to study, but at least they would fulfill some basic graduation requirements.

Within the first week or two, he had recognized enough acquaintances in his classes to work out a carpool. One day, riding down Woodward Avenue, he realized he was still noticing the seventeen clocks he had pointed out as a toddler to the women from church who had driven him to the D.O.C. He smiled to himself at the memory but said nothing to his classmates in the car.

The thing he liked best about Wayne State was finding about 20 friends from New Vine enrolled there. They began eating lunch together and meeting between classes to share. Christian fellowship at school was a new experience for Larry. It helped him feel less alone and convinced him that being a student at WSU was within God's will for him.

Janice was there, too. She and Larry took several classes together during the first two years, and she was happy to take lecture notes for him and help in other ways. Between classes they slipped little messages to each other, continuations of whatever conversation they might have had the day before.

> Larry,
>
> I want you to know that I am praying for you and your relationship with Skip. God is in control. He can make Skip's heart understand your heart. Try to look at Skip through the eyes of Jesus. Jesus loves both of you. Remember how relationships are supposed to go through trials, to make them stronger and closer. This could be what is happening. Trust in our Lord. He's good.
>
> > And I care
> > and I love you too
> > In Sonshine,
> > Janice

New Vine Community emphasized being brothers and sisters in Christ. They also emphasized expressing God's love to each other. But these were young adults in New Vine, with the normal young adult longings. Sometimes the lines between expressing God's love and expressing personal love can become blurred. Larry fell in love with Janice.

They had been driving for miles that moonlit night. Now Larry parked on a hilltop overlooking the twinkling lights of a western suburb. He shut off the ignition and turned to Janice.

"We've known each other for a year and a half now, been really close. We started out as brother and sister, but I think we've become even more than that in the last few weeks."

"Oh, Larry, our relationship in Christ is so beautiful and so important to me. Please don't spoil it by getting serious!"

He thought a minute. Then, bluntly, he asked, "Is it my handicap?"

"No! Oh no!" Janice exclaimed. "Of course it isn't! Surely you know better than that!"

He gripped the steering wheel in the silent car. She sat hunched against the door, her unhappy eyes pleading with him to understand.

Then an analogy came to his mind. He turned to her, speaking softly, carefully. "Our bodies are like cars. Some people go through life in a fine sedan, some in a sleek sports car. You have a luxury model," he sighed appreciatively. "But mine is an old clunker. Some people drive smoothly through life, while I go clattering down the road. But when we get to Heaven, my body will be just as good as anyone else's. In fact, I'll probably be a Cadillac then."

"I'm sure you will. That's great, Larry. But that's not the point. The point is," she went on earnestly, "that I think of you as my brother. I feel very close to you. I can tell you all my problems and count on you to help me through. But getting romantic would spoil all that. Please, let's just go on the way we've been. I love you, Larry, but as a brother."

And he had to be satisfied with that. He did date during the college years, and some relationships were more romantic than others. He kept Janice in the back of his mind, but they drifted further apart. Eventually she married someone else.

New Vine had branched out beyond the Friday night prayer and praise service and the weekly classes. The community had bought a couple of old houses in Detroit and formed "households," communal living in which each person gave everything he had to the house. Their days began and ended with prayer, and they lived together as a family. The whole group, led by the household "father," decided who would go to college and who would work to provide financial support.

While in high school, Larry longed to become part of a New Vine household. There were several reasons that he didn't. A major one was that he wasn't physically capable of independent living at that point. Another was that he didn't feel that God was calling him to do that, at least for the time being. The most important reason was the feeling God wanted him to remain active in First Presbyterian Church of Royal Oak.

He struggled often with the tension between New Vine and his church. At that age, he was no longer discussing problems with his parents. He turned to Jeni and Dick Wiggers, a couple who were advisors for Senior High Fellowship and good friends of the Patton family. One discussion lasted a whole afternoon:

"I'm considering leaving the church and being totally a part of New Vine," Larry announced.

"Oh, really? Why would you want to do that?" Dick asked cautiously.

"Let's face it—all my spiritual growth is coming from New Vine, not from the church. I often wonder what would have happened to me if Paul Irwin hadn't cared enough to take me to New Vine. What kind of spiritual life would I have now? Maybe none!"

Jeni handed him a glass of lemonade with one of the flexible straws she kept on hand for his visits. She and Dick understood what Larry was feeling. It was something the members of the adult Bible study group had often experienced. The membership of First Presbyterian Church was large, and most of them were not "turned-on Christians." Those who *were* often felt discouraged and overwhelmed by the majority. Their growth, like Larry's in New Vine, had come through small group Bible study, prayer, and fellowship. It was tempting to break away and turn their backs on the church.

"Yeah, but let's think about that for a minute. How did you

know Paul Irwin?" Dick asked, knowing the answer.

"Through the church," Larry admitted.

"Right. What if he had left the church and become totally a part of New Vine? Who would have taken you down there?"

"And you went with him, Larry," Jeni added, "because he was a leader in Senior High Fellowship that you looked up to and respected. That was two or three years ago. Now you are looked up to for being a spiritual leader in the Senior High Fellowship and in Our Group" [the college age Bible study group].

Dick hammered the point home, "What if all the strong Christians decided to leave our church? No one would be left to teach and to help other members in their spiritual growth."

So Larry continued his active role at First Presbyterian Church. He didn't feel good about it at the time, but he was convinced that it was God's will for him. The tension between the church and New Vine would continue.

But he did move away from home, into a Halfway House with five other young men from New Vine, although it was not an official "household."

Steve tells about his brother's achievement in a paper he wrote for his senior English class:

More Than An Average Guy

My brother, Larry, moved out of our house a few months ago to live with some friends in Detroit, and even though I joked about loving to see him leave, I really hated for him to go. He has meant a lot to me, and my parents, more than just any average brother or son because what he has accomplished over the years has been harder for him than for the typical boy growing up. For you see, my brother is physically handicapped. He was born with cerebral palsy and has had a handicap with weak muscles all his life. Living with a handicapped person has been very difficult, but in the end I will have gained so much more that when I look back I consider myself very lucky to have had a brother like Larry.

Growing up with Larry has been hard, with him receiving all the attention because of his illness. He has gotten many of the things he has wanted throughout his life and been given things that he has needed, though he is not spoiled. I've had to do many things for him, such as tying his shoes, buttoning his clothes, fixing his meals, and cleaning up for him when he made a mess, which have been very trying, but very profitable. Helping Larry over the years has made me feel wonderful when I see the things that he can do now.

Larry has accomplished many things that people, including doctors, have said were impossible for people with his handicap. Probably the first thing that Larry accomplished was being able to walk without crutches or braces on his legs. There was a time when he always had to have them on, but he worked hard and after a few years was able to take them off for good. This produced a moment of joy for him as well as the rest of us, but he wasn't going to stop there.

As he became older he got more and more use from his muscles and learned to do many things. One day came when he learned to do something that had to be a minor miracle. He had learned how to ride a bike just as well as anyone else.

I can say, though, that he was hardly content with riding a bike. He later wanted to move on to bigger and better things. He wanted to drive a car. We were skeptical at first. I was a skeptic for a long time, but when I first rode in a driver's education car with Larry behind the wheel, I was amazed. This was Larry, my brother with cerebral palsy, driving on the right side of the road as calmly as could be. I couldn't believe that he was driving an automobile, but he later went on to receive a driver's license with no restrictions.

Larry still does many things which amaze more and more people all the time, but I have learned that he can do just about anything he sets his mind to. He has gotten all the attention over the years, and it has been rough having to wait on him all the time, but it has brought happiness to me to see his accomplishments and know that it was all worth it.

So when Larry left home, six months after graduation from high school, while attending Wayne State University, even though we were saddened, it has brought us joy because he was being able to move away from home and start a new life of miracles without the aid of his parents being there to take care of him.

There were five young men, all college students, in this Halfway House of New Vine, and they had been together two months before Larry joined them. Their schedule of assigned duties was set, and a group feeling had developed. How would a sixth person fit in at this point?

Morning prayers were at 7:00 because the first one to leave for the day had to depart at 7:30. They teased Larry about his having to be dragged out of bed every morning. During the day, each went his own way. Every afternoon someone was scheduled to prepare dinner, and other work duties were also assigned. They helped each other with school work and had evening prayers about 10 P.M.

Larry couldn't prepare dinners, but he helped with table setting, cleanup, and other duties. He appreciated Dave's help with his calculus course work. After he had lived there for about a month, someone said at evening prayers, "Larry, it seems as if you've been here since Day One!"

Larry glowed. What a great feeling to be accepted and appreciated by the other guys!

But by August things weren't working out as well as before. The house was sold, so Larry and the other young men moved home again, temporarily. New Vine was becoming more ingrown, asking for greater commitment from the members, and many were uncomfortable with that.

In the fall of '76, at one of the New Vine Tuesday night meetings, the leader said to the whole group, "We feel you're wasting your energies in two jobs."

Somehow, Larry knew what was coming. He had lived with the tension between New Vine and First Presbyterian Church for five years. Currently at church he was teaching the fourth, fifth, and sixth grade with the Bitzers. He had committed himself not only for Sunday mornings but also for one afternoon and evening per week. The children came to church about 5 P.M. for games and crafts, then a light supper, followed by prayer and Bible study.

The New Vine leader went on talking about how members needed to concentrate their time and energies in New Vine, to further their own spiritual growth. Then they adjourned to their small-group classes where the discussion continued.

There, Jim said, "We leaders have prayed about this, and we're asking you tonight to decide. Will you give yourself 100% to New Vine? Are you ready to make that commitment? If not, then you can no longer be part of the Community."

Larry was stunned. *New Vine has been my life for the last five years! I expected it always would be. I can't turn my back on it. But how can I turn my back on my church?* He thought of the children, the Bitzers, the Senior High Fellowship, and Our Group. He had made commitments. And, of course, there was his family.

There was a time of prayer, in which each member of the small group searched his soul. Then Jim asked each one individually. Larry's eyes burned with tears. Then it was his turn.

"Larry," Jim asked, "are you with us or not?"

With profound sadness, Larry shook his head. "I can't," he murmured. Part of his life had just died. He left the room and New Vine. He was out. He never went back.

Within a little more than a year, New Vine disbanded. They sold their houses and had garage sales to dispose of the contents. Larry bought the tapes of all the classes.

Meanwhile, the struggle with VRS went on.

COUNSELORS CASE REPORT

12-16-75 CASE INFORMATION
Counselor saw client on this date. Client attended spring and fall quarter at Wayne State University in 1975. Client maintained an average grade in three classes in the fall quarter. Larry stated that Betsy Ferris helps him complete examinations which require no time limit on

mathematics tests. Client will take four classes
next term which include humanities, two
mathematics courses and political science.
Counselor has sent for transcript from Wayne
State. Client has questioned again possibility of
financial assistance from VRS for college.
Counselor emphasized that this agency does not
feel this plan is a feasible one for client. Client
will work in the maintenance department with
Parks and Recreation for the city of Berkley during the summer. His lapidary hobby of rocks has
earned client $800 in profit. Counselor stressed
some career exploration in this area, and client
might attend a rock class in the summer.

Larry had always liked rocks. In third and fourth grades,
he had brought home every loose rock in the neighborhood.
Finally Bill had seen enough! As Larry wrote an autobiogra-
phical paper in junior high:

"Another hobby is collecting rocks. Rocks are
coming out my ears, I have so many. I can
remember when I had about six garbage cans full
of big and little rocks. My dad had to take out
the back seat and put rocks in. He took them to
the dump. I hope to be able to set up a rock
laboratory. Right now I do not have the money."

The Christmas before his fifteenth birthday, his parents gave
him a rock polisher, something he had wanted for a long time.
Then he began visiting rock shops, and on family trips he
spent a lot of time chiseling or digging rocks. When he had
cut and polished several stones, Bill helped him by mount-
ing them in fittings. Soon Larry had enough rock jewelry to
open a booth at the annual Berkley Flea Market.

Over a period of five years or so, he had earned about $1000 from his hobby, but "hobby" was all it ever was. Larry never seriously considered making a living from rocks. Besides the fact that he wasn't all that interested, there was the problem of manual dexterity. Bill had done all the fine work for him. Larry's hands weren't capable of gluing the stones into the fittings.

Yet this was the vocational plan that VRS considered most feasible for Larry, even after he had successfully completed a year and a half at Wayne State.

In the summer of '76, two exciting events occurred. Larry decided to go to the Fellowship of Christian Athletes camp. Bill was on the staff that week. He and Sue had been going to FCA camp for three or four years. Larry was reluctant to go because he hadn't been active in sports since high school, but he finally agreed.

His group of ten, called a huddle, was made up of young men who took sports almost as seriously as they took their Christian faith. Larry worked as hard as he could just to hold his own and not hold back his huddle.

Two days into the camp schedule, the Schinnick Sweepstakes was held. This consists of several relay events, and each person in a huddle does an event for his team. Larry was to run the last 100 yards.

His huddle had a good 50 yard lead when he was handed the baton. He gradually worked up speed in the lane, and then he felt the smooth stick slide into his waiting hand. He ran as fast as he could, his feet pounding the track and the blood pounding in his ears. Several runners passed him before he crossed the finish line. He had lost the Sweepstakes for his huddle!

But before he could give in to despair, his entire huddle ran to the finish line, picked him up, and carried him off, congratulating him for his attempt.

The director of the camp, Dick Shilts, turned away with

tears in his eyes. Seeing Larry give his all in that last event and seeing the response of the other members of the huddle suddenly clarified for Dick what Christian athletics was all about: giving your all for the team and caring more about your teammates than about winning. When he saw those highly competitive athletes treating Larry, the kid who had lost the race for them, like a hero, he saw a transformation accomplished by team spirit and love. *That's what FCA is all about, and I've never seen it so clearly before!* he mused.

The closing night of the five-day camp, an awards night was held. Larry's huddle ended up second, over-all, for the week. He had longed for a trophy to put alongside Steve's gleaming collection, but there were no trophies given for second place. As the evening progressed, with singing and short talks, Larry realized trophies were not important after all— God was!

Then, after all the other awards, Dick Shilts said, "I have one more award to give out, one that has never before been given. It is for the Athlete of the Week. This award is given to one who has put all he had into every event, who has exemplified the true competitive spirit of athletics, and who has deepened everyone's understanding of the application of our Christian faith to our love of sports. Will Larry Patton please come forward!"

Before Larry could even look up, athletes were standing on their chairs, applauding. His parents had tears running down their cheeks. He was sitting three rows from the back and had a long, long walk ahead of him. Half dazed, he made his way to the stage with tears in his eyes.

Clutching his trophy, he went outside to thank God and to promise to use it for His glory. Then his huddle surrounded him, hugging and pounding him on the back.

"Guys, I'm so full of joy and praise for God, I feel like running the 100-yard dash again!" Larry exclaimed.

"All right!"

"Why not!"

And before he knew it, they had lifted him over the ten-foot fence of the football field and clambered over, themselves. The whole huddle ran the 100-yard dash at midnight and finished with a prayer meeting, singing "Father Abraham" at the top of their lungs.

16

Steps Toward Independence

Right after FCA camp, Bill and Sue left for a two-week trip to New England. While they were gone, Larry and his friend Scott Jones decided to look for an apartment together. They looked at one after another and finally found one that pleased both of them. It was in Royal Oak, and the rent was $230 a month. Larry phoned his parents in Vermont.

"Hey, Mom, I'm moving out. I found a two-bedroom apartment with Scott. It's $230 a month. We gotta make the decision before you get home. Okay?"

"Larry! $230 a month! We paid only $95 for our apartment!"

"That was 20 years ago, Mom. This is 1976. What do you say?"

"No!"

"Mom, we need it. It's a gorgeous apartment!"

"I'll bet it is! No, you wait till we get home."

Larry was "stirred up like crazy" until they finally got home. Even then they refused to decide immediately. Instead, as was their custom, Bill and Sue presented the situation to their prayer group.

Pam and Gary Moultrup were members of the group at that time. Though they lived in Detroit, they were advisors of the Senior High Fellowship at First Presbyterian Church in Royal Oak. They were only a couple of years older than Larry.

"The flat below us is for rent," Gary said.

"That's right," Pam agreed. "The landlord's son has been living there, and he's just gotten married and moved out. I think the rent is $150 a month."

Since Bill and Sue would have to pay Larry's half of the rent, that figure sounded much better than $230. And they felt more comfortable having good Christian friends just upstairs over Larry and Scott.

The next day Larry went to see the apartment. It was great! He drove to where Scott was working to tell him about it. Scott liked the apartment. So did his parents. A couple of weeks later, Larry and Scott moved in.

They had no furniture, so the landlord sold them all the furnishings, including a washer and dryer, for only $200.

For six months Larry and Scott shared the apartment and had some good times together. Then Scott lost his job and had to move back home. Larry lived there a month alone, yet not completely independent. Pam and Gary were upstairs, ready to help as needed.

Then came John, a friend of Janice's. That, too, was a compatible arrangement. It lasted only four and a half months, however, because John planned to get married. This time Larry was the one to move, to share an apartment with Steve Hull, a friend from Our Group. This apartment was across town, though still in Detroit. Steve and Larry dated two girls from Our Group. Then Steve, too, decided to marry, and Larry was alone again.

All of these episodes were steps toward independent living.

In the summer of 1977, while working again for Berkley Parks and Recreation, Larry began to explore the possibilities of getting a co-op job. This was a program Wayne State supervised with private companies in the Detroit area. A student would work, for example, during the winter and summer quarters and take classes at WSU for the spring and fall terms.

There were many benefits. While working, the student earned not only wages but also credit toward graduation. If his work performance were satisfactory, he was practically assured of a job with that company after graduation, if he chose. If he preferred to work elsewhere, the work experience gave him an advantage over other graduates who had had only academic training.

Larry had interviews with three companies. Bill and Sue prayed with him before each appointment, asking God to help the potential employer understand Larry's speech and to give Larry confidence. They concluded each prayer with a commitment to trust Him for whatever His will was for Larry.

The first three interviews failed to produce a job. Larry was discouraged, but the head of the co-op program at WSU assured him that his experience was typical for all students, not just handicapped ones.

At this point, Steve had completed two years at WSU on a scholarship which would have paid nearly all his expenses for the full four years. However, the best course of study for him seemed to be at University of Michigan, so he transferred and lost the scholarship.

The full expenses of two college students were a heavy load for Bill and Sue. So that summer they turned again to the Vocational Rehabilitation Services for financial aid.

COUNSELORS CASE REPORT

7-6-77 CASE INFORMATION

Client was seen with parents this date. His mother believes that client has proved his success in the computer field by his 3.11 overall grade point average. He currently has taken 107 credits and needs 180 credits to graduate. Client received the following grades during the spring term:

Computer Science, A, Art History, A, and Geology, B; which total 13 credits. Parents want VRS to decide by the end of the month if they will financially support this program. Parents' financial situation has changed because another son has transferred to the University of Michigan and will receive no financial assistance. Client has continued his remedial reading program at Midwestern Resource Center for the past three years. Client qualifies for a co-op program at Wayne, working and attending school at the same time. Ms. Shrauder [Betsy Ferris] will explore a job at Chrysler and City of Detroit for a student assistant in Computer Programming. This job should determine client's abilities in the field. Client still reads his own tests and someone else writes the answers. He writes his own computer program by hand and types it directly on the terminal.

Larry's discouragement with the job interviews shows up in the next entry of the VRS records.

COUNSELORS CASE REPORT

7-13-77 CASE INFORMATION

Counselor contacted client this date. Client rejected the plan to be evaluated at Rehabilitation Institute to determine his functional capabilities on a job. He stated that he "has been through enough garbage." He was refused a job with the city of Detroit, and Chrysler, because they did not believe that he had the physical abilities for the job. VRS has no current medical informa-

tion on client (latest information is dated 1973).
Current transcript is included in the casefile.
Client will meet with Mr. Johnson and this
counselor on July 25 at 4:30 P.M.

It must be said that VRS did actively investigate Larry's
case. On July 28, the counselor talked with Dr. Helper, the
professor at WSU who had taught PL 1, a computer language
class which determines if a student can handle a computer
science program. Larry's grade had been a high B, with a
91 on the final exam. According to Professor Helper, Larry
appeared to be an adequate candidate for the computer field.

They checked with Dr. Ambinder about Larry's progress
at the reading clinic. They learned that in three years, his
reading level had risen from fifth to tenth grade. Then the
VRS record questioned the validity of Larry's grade point
average of 3.1 if his reading level were so low.

They checked with Mike Liefkofsky, a person with CP who
had worked as a computer programmer for Wayne State for
twelve years. He explained to VRS the various aspects of a
computer programmer's job and told them he believed they
were being too critical of Larry. But still, VRS thought Larry's
vocational plan was not realistic enough for them to support.

Finally, completely frustrated and outraged, Sue went to
the local office of their Congressman, Rep. James Blanchard.

"This is a tax-supported agency," she emphasized. "Their
purpose is to help handicapped people get the training they
need to become self-supporting. But except for some financial help with the reading clinic, all Larry has had from them
has been discouragement. Not only that, they have belittled
him and his chances for success in spite of all the input from
'experts'! I think you need to look into this agency to see how
they are fulfilling the mandate the government has given
them."

She received this reply:

Dear Sue:

Thank you for stopping by my home office. I am sorry to learn of the difficulties that your son has experienced regarding the Vocational Rehabilitation Service.

I have contacted Mr. Don Johnson, District Supervisor of the VRS in Royal Oak. Mr. Johnson informed me that a favorable decision was made by the VRS for support of the program at Wayne State University that Larry will be attending. This decision is termed an extended evaluation and the commitment by VRS is for one year.

At the end of that time, VRS will review their decision.

The decision at that time will be based on what has transpired during the year.

Mr. Johnson further informed me that there will be conditions to this decision and Larry will be receiving a letter from Mr. Johnson stating those conditions.

The following day, Larry received a three-page letter from Mr. Johnson which said, in part:

Dear Larry:

I am writing to inform you of the decision made to assist you in your program at Wayne State University during the coming year. We are genuinely pleased to rule in your favor and certainly hope that you will continue through to successful completion of the program and employment. We will be available to assist you in every way possible, although the primary responsibility for completion of the program rests with you; a responsibility you and your family have already accepted.

The next three paragraphs note the positive and negative factors VRS considered in reaching this decision. Then Mr. Johnson continued,

> Essentially, in my judgement the evidence is inconclusive, pointing neither to success nor to failure. Since, however, you bring to the situation excellent personal motivation, strong family support and since you have completed 2+ years at Wayne State University with a 3.01 GPA, I have made the decision to support your program. This means that you will have available financial support of the agency (as defined in the Department's College Policy with the University Financial Aid Office).
>
> I would be less than responsible if I did not note my serious concerns about the plan and program you are in. In so doing, I do not mean to discourage you or to intimate "I told you so," but only to offer my observations to guide you in your vocational development. It is my opinion that the remaining higher level classes in math and particularly in computer science, will be most difficult and may eventually cause you to change your plans. Additionally, unless you are able to demonstrate competitive and timely skills in interacting with the computer, a placement on a job will be most difficult to consummate and may not be possible in a competitive setting. . .
>
> Please do not interpret our position to be one that does not have faith in you or one that will not engage in a "risk." We are working with numerous clients for whom there is no guarantee of success and in fact have been encouraged by Congress to do so. We sincerely hope that you

> will be successful and we will do all we can to
> assist you. Should your wishes not materialize
> and the computer program be found unattainable
> we certainly will be available to assist you in
> developing alternative plans. . .

For the remainder of his college career, Larry received from VRS an average of $12.50 per week for transportation and lunches. Welcome though it was, that was the full extent of their financial assistance. The checks for $150 per quarter arrived at the end of each term, and VRS couldn't make it retroactive.

17

IBM

While looking for a co-op job, Larry remembered his meeting with Norm Henry of IBM more than three years earlier. He asked his mother to phone Mr. Henry. She gladly agreed and made the call promptly.

"This is Sue Patton," she said. "Do you remember when Mrs. Giffin, Mrs. Ludwig, and Larry and I came to see you at the IBM Data Center? Well, Larry is now a student at Wayne State, majoring in math and computer science. We were wondering if IBM had any co-op jobs that he might apply for."

"Of course I remember you, Mrs. Patton," Mr. Henry replied. "Larry wants a co-op job, does he? We don't have any co-op programs, but we might work out something. I'd like to see Larry again before deciding. What is he doing this summer?"

"Working for Berkley Parks and Rec. He could probably take a day off . . ."

"No, no! We don't want him to miss any work. Does he come home for lunch?"

"He could."

"All right, why don't I meet him at your home during his lunch break next Thursday. Would that work out?"

"Fine. He'll be here about 11:30."

The following Thursday when Bill and Larry drove up, they found a big Cadillac parked in the driveway. Larry looked down at his work T-shirt, cut-off jeans, and gym shoes. *Uh-oh. I'm really prepared for an interview.* They went in and found not one but two men attired in three-piece business suits. Mr. Henry had brought along Voris Conrad, the sales manager who had worked with several handicapped people at IBM, to help him decide whether Larry would be employable.

The men shook hands with Larry and then they all sat down, Mr. Henry, Mr. Conrad, Bill, Sue, and Larry, at the dinette table. The others drank iced tea while Larry ate his lunch, and they talked about IBM's training program.

"Shortly after coming aboard, our employees are sent to New York for training. Would you like to go to New York, Larry?"

He looked from Mr. Conrad to Mr. Henry and then at his parents. "Yeah, I'd go to New York," he said bravely.

He didn't know that before he arrived they had asked Sue if Larry was capable of independent living and travel. Because of his experience with various roommates and the gaps between roommates, she was able to assure the men from IBM that he could. *Thank you, God,* she prayed silently, *for bringing Larry to this point.*

The five of them talked a little longer, the Pattons ill at ease with these important business executives in their little house. Larry was trying extra hard to eat carefully. Then, suddenly, Mr. Conrad spilled his tea! Sue hurried to clean it up, of course, but in the flurry, she and Larry exchanged quick glances. Thank goodness it hadn't been Larry's accident! The tension for the Pattons was mercifully broken.

The conversation about IBM went on, and then it was time for Larry to return to work. "Thanks for coming out to talk to me," he said.

"It's good to see you again, Larry," Mr. Henry said. "We'll be in touch."

About three weeks later, Larry was called to the IBM office

to take the aptitude test required of everyone who interviews with the company. Bill went with him, waiting in the office and observing everything. While Larry took the test, Norm Henry told Bill that Larry had the job.

Larry didn't know that, of course. The week before, he had had a promising interview with Burroughs, but IBM was certainly his first choice.

Usually it takes three weeks to score that test; this time it took just ten minutes. Mr. Henry told Larry his score was average and that was good. The conversation continued, but Mr. Henry wasn't saying the magic words. Finally, with the brazen gall of youth, Larry asked, "Are you interested, because Burroughs wants an answer."

Bill was aghast. Mr. Henry merely smiled and said, "We want you to start at $4 an hour, as soon as you can."

I'm gonna die! Larry thought. *I've struck gold!* But with exquisite aplomb he said, "I'll let you know."

Of course he accepted. He gave Parks and Rec a few days' notice and then took some time off to buy new clothes, because Mr. Henry had said, "You will wear a button-front shirt; you will wear a tie. You will be a part of the office like everyone else."

So he bought white dress shirts. Mom removed the top three buttons and stitched them over buttonholes. Then she sewed tiny Velcro patches under the buttonholes and on the spots where the buttons had been. Larry bought clip-on ties and conservative suits.

A week and a half later, the transformation from Parks and Rec maintenance worker to young business man complete, Larry went to work at IBM. It was Wednesday after Labor Day, 1977.

Mr. Conrad met him, talked to him for a while, and introduced him to everyone in the office. He settled Larry at a desk and gave him a book to read, and later took him to lunch. Another manager went along. Larry tried hard to make a good impression.

He did very well until dessert, apple pie served on lightweight plastic plates. Larry's fork hit the edge of the plate, which caromed across the table to Mr. Conrad's place.

During that split second while the pie headed in his direction, Voris Conrad thought, *Gee, wouldn't I be embarrassed if that happened to me! He probably is. If I just hand it back and say, "Think nothing of it," that probably won't set too well. We've known each other only a few days, but I've caught an inkling of a sense of humor. O God, please let this be the right thing to do.* So, meeting Larry's horrified gaze, with a twinkle in his eye, Voris picked up his fork, said "Thank you," and took a bite of Larry's pie!

Larry let out a yelp, "It's mine!"

The three of them laughed as Voris returned the pie. The tension was broken, and what might have been one of Larry's most embarrassing moments became a joke that they still laugh about.

The first co-op stint lasted until the end of September. During that month, Larry had worked his way through some self-study books about the company and had become acquainted with the office personnel and routine. Then he went to school full-time for the fall quarter, returned to IBM for the winter term, and back to school for the spring quarter. During the summer, he worked full-time for IBM.

Reflecting on that year, Voris Conrad says, "Getting kids involved, *especially* handicapped kids, in a co-op environment in college is really a tremendous way to get started. The employer is just as afraid as the handicapped prospective employee. The first interaction is bound to be full of tension for both of them.

"The beautiful part of co-op is that they can have it in little doses. They can have a chance to see each other and feel each other out and then go away for a few weeks. Everyone gets a chance to re-evaluate, to say, 'I did that wrong.' 'That was dumb.' So they have at it again for another two or three months. And a whole lot of good things come out.

"First, the prospective employer doesn't have to be afraid he's made a life-long commitment, so he can be a little more at ease. 'Geez, it's only going to last three months.' [IBM has a policy of never firing an employee, so of course they are very careful in hiring.]

"Second, the prospective worker has a chance to be involved on an inter-active basis in the business world in small pieces. It's his first job. Maybe three months is all he wants to take at one time. Other employees may be looking at him, staring. He needs three months to think about 'Maybe I could do that better.' 'Did I handle that right?' 'Did I do my part making them feel comfortable around me?' And then go back and do that again. So that is a great way for people with handicaps to get involved in the business world."

It certainly was for Larry. During the winter quarter he began helping full-time employees in research and "interacting with the computer," the very activity VOC Rehab had been most skeptical about his ability to do.

COUNSELOR CASE REPORT

3-21-78 CASE INFORMATION

Client was seen at IBM on 3-17-78 with the employer, Mr. Conrad. Client completed the basic course in PL 1 (common computer language for IBM). This course consisted of 21 programs, which he completed in six weeks and received a grade of A. Client needs assistance in preparing flip charts (writing on large pads of paper) and flow charts (program system designed to explain the results to a group). Typing is not an essential in programming. If client can bridge communication gap with a dictaphone or leave his flow chart, he should be employable, according to Mr. Conrad.

Client is classified as a supplemental employee. He works with other new employees who are college graduates. Client also earns minimum wage. Mr. Conrad has not evaluated Larry in regard to independent programming. He wants to re-hire client in June to work on his own program. Mr. Conrad stated that an employer could hire Larry at less salary, and give him additional time in completing a program. Client demonstrated on the terminal a program that consisted of 400 frames, which he completed in three weeks. Mr. Conrad stated that this was competitive time. The employer stated that some independent data processing companies hire women and students for part-time employment.

Client will continue his co-op program in June. He will enroll in the spring program at WSU. Client will forward recent transcript to us.

Not only was Larry gaining valuable experience; he was also making friends. The IBM office at that time was located just a mile from the WSU campus, so even during his academic quarters, Larry often dropped in at IBM just to say hello or to meet someone for lunch. In addition, he asked Voris' advice about what classes he should enroll in at Wayne and then concentrated on the areas Voris suggested. He did well at school and well at IBM.

Larry continued to have difficulty with Voc Rehab. The promised financial aid did not come during the summer quarter of '78. When he told Voris about it, Voris was hearing a familiar story. Other people had told him of problems with that agency. So with the permission of the Pattons, Voris went right to the top, the state office of the Bureau of Vocational Rehabilitation, with a letter of his own on December 6, 1978. It led to an investigation of the Royal Oak office of VRS. Larry finally received the summer '78 funds during the winter '79 quarter.

After working co-op in winter and summer quarters of 1978, Larry had been a college student for four years and still had several credits to take before graduating. So, acting on Voris' advice and his own inclinations, he decided to attend classes for three consecutive quarters, beginning with fall, 1978, so he could graduate the next June. He did work for IBM during his three-week Christmas vacation.

One day very early in March, Larry dropped in at IBM to say hello. Everyone he saw said, "Voris wants to see you, so don't leave."

Larry waited and waited, but Voris was out. Finally Larry said to the secretary, "I really have to leave. Tell Voris to call me."

He got in the elevator and rode down to the first floor. As the elevator doors parted, Voris walked in the front of the building. Spying Larry, he called, "Turn around. Get back in that elevator. Get right back up to the office."

"But I'm late, Voris," Larry protested as his boss joined him in the cabled cage.

Upstairs, Voris led Larry into his office and shut the door.

"I really have to leave," Larry pleaded.

Already busy with papers at his desk, Voris looked up to say, "What would you like to start at?"

"What?!" Finally Larry realized he was talking salary, so he said, "Seventeen thousand dollars."

"If I gave you sixteen, would you take it?"

Larry collapsed into a chair. "Would I take it! Give it to me!"

"All right. You've got yourself a Letter." [In June, Larry got the Letter of Employment, saying he would start at that salary on July 2, 1979, signed by IBM.]

Larry sat there weakly. *Here I am here sitting here with the guy I've been working for for the last two years, and this is it. No formal interview, and I have a permanent job with IBM.*

Voris was still busy with his papers. Finally he looked up again with a smile and said, "That's all I wanted. See you later."

Larry was jubilant. He couldn't wait to tell Mom and Dad, and especially Voc Rehab.

The letter he received from that office about a week later reflects the fall-out from Voris' letter to Lansing as well as Larry's news of the job offer from IBM.

Dear Larry:

This is by way of confirming the discussion we had on February 8, 1979, in Royal Oak. As I indicated, several factors led to the difficulties our agency experienced in serving you and your dissatisfaction with our services. It is clear that we did not give early enough or sufficient weight to your unique ability and that we were overly influenced by past failures with clients having similar disabilities. Additionally, the assistance that you received from your parents and at school raised questions as to your true potential.

On the positive side, I think it is important to reflect on the gains that you made in agency-sponsored programs with Dr. Ambinder and their contribution to your success in college. Obviously, another ingredient for success lies with the

IBM Corporation and the opportunity they have provided you, not the least of which is the offer of a job after college.

Agency personnel involved in your case have benefitted from our review and have a deeper understanding of their role and responsibilities to assist and encourage their clients to be successful in a changing world.

I would like to extend an opportunity to you to continue to expand their understanding through work as a peer counselor with some of our staff and their clients.

Your insight should prove valuable to both the agency and our clients. Additionally, I would like to hear from you in the fall and learn about your new job and whether or not you're driving a "Camaro or a Corvette."

Your courage and forthrightness in dealing with our agency is appreciated.

18

Celebrations

For four and three-quarters years, Larry had planned not to go through Commencement at Wayne State because for that long he had felt like just a number. It was his way of declaring his individuality to say, "No, I will not be part of a herd packed into Cobo Hall Convention Arena and paraded around. I have earned my degree. You can mail my diploma."

But as the time grew closer, Mom began to apply the pressure. "Larry, it would make us so proud to see you in a cap and gown. It's a big achievement, and it deserves a public recognition."

"Nope, I'm not gonna do it!"

Then, three weeks before the ceremony, he decided to do it, for her. He ordered cap and gown and tickets and picked up the invitations.

That evening he went to his parents' house and dropped the invitations in Mom's lap. "There. There you are. Send 'em to whoever you want to come."

"You mean you're going through with it after all? Oh, Larry, have you just been tormenting me all this time?"

"No. I just changed my mind. What's for supper here? Got enough for me, too?"

The night of graduation, the Patton family and Mrs. Wall went early to Cobo Hall down near the river in Detroit. The floor of the arena was filled with chairs for the 8000 graduates. One section on each side was reserved for faculty members. A platform at the front held seats for about twenty dignitaries, a lectern, large baskets of flowers, the Wayne State flag on one side and the United States flag on the other. At strategically located spots on the arena floor were stands with rolled sheets of white paper tied with green ribbons. Actual diplomas were sent out by mail. The rest of the arena had non-reserved seats for families and friends of the graduates.

The Wayne State University Band filled the vast hall with ringing march music as the endless procession of graduates filed in. Larry was seated far to one side, three rows from the back. Again he had a long walk ahead of him.

During the conferring of doctoral and graduate degrees, he scanned the crowd, looking for his family. Two rows up, just to his left, he spotted a familiar face. It was Marsha Snider, his academic teacher from Tyler. He was sure it was only a coincidence that had brought her to his graduation. No doubt one of her family was receiving a degree of some kind, but it was neat to have her there. *It's like a circle,* he thought. *She was in on the beginning, and here she is at the end.*

Finally, nearly an hour and a half after the processional, it was time for conferring Bachelor of Science in Computer Science. There were only sixteen graduates in that category. As Larry bobbed past, tassel flying, Marsha Snider recognized him, and she, too, was happy to be present for Larry's graduation.

At the stand for their group, the dean handed nameless graduates the imitation diplomas. Eyes did not meet; hands did not touch. It was an assembly line—the degree mill. But when the nameless man saw Larry working his way across the arena floor, he wordlessly shook his hand as he gave Larry his symbol of graduation.

Sue and Bill felt that handshake as the culmination of their

years of effort to bring Larry to this point. It was the fulfillment of all that they had worked for ever since that day at
the Detroit Orthopaedic Clinic when Dr. Walsh had said, "He
has cerebral palsy." The endless exercises, the laborious school
work, the constant insistence that he do everything possible
for himself—it had all paid off. All their dreams for Larry
had been realized. When the president of the university asked
the parents of the graduates to stand for recognition for their
efforts, Sue and Bill stood up proudly. As the applause rang
out, they realized that many people had helped them arrive
at this moment, but most especially, God.

But while Bill and Sue were looking back from this pin-
nacle of achievement, Larry was looking ahead to the surprise event four days later. For a whole year now, he and Steve
had been planning a fantastic Silver Wedding Anniversary
party for their parents. And although Steve had helped with
the planning, he had been at Ann Arbor for his senior year
at the University of Michigan, so the burden of carrying out
all the plans had fallen on Larry. Not that he minded! As a
future executive, he had already learned to delegate responsibility, so he had help.

Their plans were too complicated to handle themselves.
They wanted to invite people from church, F.C.A. camp, Bible study group, and family to a feast. Of course they couldn't
afford to feed that many people. The only way they could
manage was to plan a carry-in dinner, to be held at church.
And it was to be a surprise to Bill and Sue. First Larry enlisted
Ruth Foster and Ann Dutton. Later, others were recruited.

At Christmas, Larry had "borrowed" his mother's address
book and returned it without her missing it. From that, he
sent invitations with Christmas cards to out-of-town friends
and relatives, telling them to save Saturday, June 23, for the

surprise party and asking them to respond secretly to Larry or Steve. In April, he sent printed invitations to everyone. Ann Dutton and Libby Weber agreed to receive those RSVP's and to suggest a particular covered dish to bring, to keep the menu fairly balanced. Altogether, 125 people received invitations.

All during the year, Larry and Steve dropped little hints that something big would happen on the anniversary. They encouraged Bill and Sue to plan a service of recommitment to each other and to God. Finally, things got so complicated that in March they told Bill and Sue there would be a family dinner for them at church on Saturday, June 23. That would make it easier with all the out-of-towners coming. Mom and Dad could help find places for them to stay.

Sue kept catching little clues about the plans. Ruth Foster called to say she was baking a cake and asked what kind Sue would prefer. Ruth and Mary Wall hinted of big plans and disagreements over how everything was to be handled. Larry made teasing comments. And Sue tried to pump Steve for information every time she saw him. But never did she grasp the enormity of the undertaking until the night of the party.

All day on June 23, Steve and Larry were busy. In the Fellowship Hall of the church, they set up and decorated eight tables with white paper cloths and blue crepe paper streamers. A horticulture teacher-friend of the family donated floral centerpieces for each table, a corsage for Sue, and a bouton-niere for Bill. A huge banner saying "Happy Anniversary" stretched across the stage at the front of the hall.

Larry and Steve had bought ham, and the cook at church donated her services to prepare it and take charge of the kitch-en. The boys had also borrowed a silver tea service, punch bowl, and candlesticks. This was to be a first-class shindig.

Bill and Sue had prepared a worship service of recommit-ment and had it printed on special programs for the "family worship service" to take place on Sunday, June 24, in the chapel. Larry and Steve had told them to get dressed up Saturday evening for the family dinner. Sue had a new dress for the occasion, and Bill wore his three-piece suit. Nervously, they waited at home for the boys to pick them up.

Finally they came, and all four drove off. There were several joking comments about the dinner that night and the worship service Sunday. Larry pulled up to the back door of the church, hidden from the parking lot.

Bill and Sue followed the boys in the back door, down the steps toward the rear entrance of the Fellowship Hall. Bill noticed many pairs of feet in the Hall as he descended the stairs, but Sue chattered away, oblivious.

The boys held open the door, Bill and Sue stepped in, and 70 voices yelled, "Surprise! Happy Anniversary!" Twenty flash bulbs flared, capturing the astonishment of the happy couple's faces just before the tears erupted.

It took a while to greet all those guests! The greatest surprises were Jeni and Dick Wiggers, who had moved to Atlanta just a few days earlier for Dick to enter seminary and had flown back to help Bill and Sue celebrate this anniversary. And there were Don and Leslie Wharton, Fellowship of Christian Athletes camp friends! Don, a composer-musician, had given a concert a couple of months earlier, and Sue had said to them, "I wish you could come to our anniversary party, but I know you have to be in Pennsylvania for the FCA conference that weekend." How had they managed to be here tonight?

Larry and Steve gave their parents a chance to greet all their friends briefly, and then Larry took over as master of ceremonies. "Now that you've said hello to everyone, let's eat before it gets cold!" Craig Davies, the assistant minister, asked the blessing, and then everyone filled their plates.

As they sat at the head table with their sons and Sue's

parents, Sue marvelled at how well the boys had planned the party. *It's so . . . so polished! Everything is so pretty and so well done.*

But the best was yet to come.

After dinner, Larry called on Dick Wiggers to propose a toast. Then Don Wharton played his guitar and sang. Next, a projector screen was lowered under the banner on the stage, the lights were darkened, and a slide/tape show was presented by Lin Buckindail. Larry had gone through the family collection of slides without his parents knowing it and filched 200 slides for Lin's project. Lin had put 30 of them together with a hilarious narration spanning the 25 years of marriage.

She ended with this tribute, "Dearest Bill and Sue, it is on this most special occasion that we gather together to wish you all of life's best. Your friends respect and need you; your family loves you more dearly than you could ever know; your sons say 'Thank you for the loving care, for life itself.' God bless you and keep you both together forever!"

Gifts were presented: Sue's baby shoes which Mrs. Wall had uncovered in a recent move, (the boys filled them with air plants because Mom was no good with caring for the "real" plants) and a framed collage of family pictures.

Through it all, Sue's only regret was that the recommitment service they had planned was scheduled for the following day. How appropriate it would have been to do it tonight with all their dear friends here.

Just then, Larry, the master of ceremonies, said, "This concludes this portion of the program. Now we'd like to invite all of you to come upstairs to the chapel where Craig Davies and Bob Miller will lead our parents through a renewal of their vows. I guess an Episcopalian priest can't do much harm in a Presbyterian church," he joked.

"But the programs," Sue protested.

"They're here, Mom," Steve called to her. "I brought 'em!"

So they all went upstairs to the chapel. The organist was playing softly, and the candles were lighted. Don Wharton sang his own arrangement of I Corinthians 13, "the love chapter." Then, standing before the two ministers, flanked on either side by Larry and Steve, Bill and Sue said together, "God, we thank You that You love us and sent Jesus to die on the cross for us. We recommit our lives to You. Show us Your pathway; enable us to do your will. We give you all the praise and glory. Thank you for the 25 years we have shared, for our sons Larry and Steve, for the love and support of family and friends. We pledge our love to trust, to encourage, to strengthen, to cherish, to support, to share joys and sorrows, and to care for each other. With the help of God this will be possible."

Bob Miller closed with a prayer, and then Larry invited everyone to return to the Fellowship Hall for wedding cake. Later he thanked everyone for coming and gave centerpieces to the women who had helped make the whole event possible.

Many friends and relatives followed the Pattons home that evening. There were more gifts to unwrap and more visiting to do.

Late, late that night, Sue lay in bed waiting for sleep. Bill was already snoring softly, but she was still too excited and happy to drift off. *God is just blessing us constantly,* she mused. *This summer is the fulfillment of all we've worked so hard for, for so long. Both boys graduating from college, Larry going to work for IBM and Steve for General Motors, this wonderful party tonight, a better marriage than we started with . . . . It's all a dream come true.*

19

Take-Off

On Monday, July 2, Larry showed up for work on his first day as a full-time employee of IBM. Voris met him.

"Welcome back. Glad to have you. I got your ticket. Are your bags packed and ready to go?"

Oh boy, I'm finally going to New York to start the training program, Larry thought, but before he could respond, Voris went on.

"You're leaving in three weeks to go to California."

"California?!"

"You are going to become a PL 1 specialist. Where would be a better place for you to learn more about PL 1 than working with the PL 1 Development and Testing, where software is designed? You'll be gone three to six months."

"That makes sense." His stomach was turning flip-flops. *I'm going three thousand miles away from home for three to six months!* He knew that someday he would have to say to IBM, "I'll go wherever you want me to go," and it might as well be now. "Okay," he said.

"You'll want to leave the third weekend of July. Will that be all right?"

"No."

"No? Why?"

"I wish I could stay around until at least August 4. My best friend from high school is being married the first weekend in August, and I really want to go to his wedding. If you can't work it out, I'll skip the wedding, but I'd really like to be able to go. Also, I need to have week after next off, if possible. I'm an advisor for the Senior High Youth Fellowship at my church, and we're going on a work trip to Warren Wilson College in North Carolina."

Voris thought for a minute. There really wasn't anything much for Larry to do in the Detroit office before leaving for California. He was already familiar with the company through his co-op work, and there was no point in involving him as an assistant in anyone else's work for such a short time. Larry was going to be in California for three to six months, and obviously his commitment to this youth group was important to him. So, why not? Soon enough he would be caught up in the corporate rat race. Let him have the work trip to North Carolina and his friend's wedding.

"Okay, Larry, you can have that week off, without pay. Then let's say you'll leave August 4 for California."

"Great! I'll be ready."

Voris hesitated. He didn't want to be presumptive and have someone meet Larry in California if it weren't necessary. But he didn't want to risk not having someone meet him if the kid would feel lost. For all Voris knew, this might even be Larry's first flight. So he asked him.

"Would you like to have someone from the San Jose office meet your plane or do you want to go it alone?"

"Well, I think I'd like to have somebody meet me."

I'm glad I asked, Voris thought.

Then Larry went on, "It's just been recently I've gotten past the stage of being real upset about people looking at me. I still have a little trouble with that. I'd feel more comfortable if I knew there'd be someone there that could help me."

"Okay, sure. I'll arrange it," Voris promised. *Walk a mile in my moccasins,* he thought. *I wonder how many other fears he never mentions.*

The week of the work camp at Warren Wilson College in North Carolina with the senior highs was a good one. Each day the kids worked hard, doing some maintenance work on the college grounds in the morning and leading a vacation church school in the afternoons. In the evenings were devotional times of Bible study and prayer, led by Larry and the other advisors.

On Thursday, for a special treat, the group from Michigan took a bus trip to the legendary Sliding Rock. Riding along on the Blue Ridge Parkway, they crossed and re-crossed a bubbling mountain stream. Fifty miles or so from the college, the bus driver turned off to the right to a public parking lot. Just in front of them, that mountain stream widened, coursed over a huge, smooth rock, and plunged into a deep pool fifteen or twenty feet below. There, strung on deep-set metal poles, ropes led from the edge of the pool to the paved sidewalks on either side. The stream burbled on under a footbridge and back out to chase the Parkway down the mountain.

The Michigan group watched as several people wearing jeans or cut-off shorts waded into the stream, sat down at the top of Sliding Rock, pushed off, and slid, screaming all the way, into the pool below. From there, they quickly splashed to the side, ran up the ramp, and did it again. Wasting no time, the young people jumped into the water and joined the fun.

Their sponsors watched from the benches along the sidewalk, perfectly contented to enjoy the experience vicariously.

"How cold do you suppose that water is?"

"Probably no colder than Lake Huron."

"I don't know. It's snow-melt, surely."

"I notice no one stays in the pool very long."

"You wouldn't either, with more people sliding in all the

time."

One after another the kids slithered down, shrieking and splashing. "C'mon," they yelled at their advisors watching from the upper bank. "It's fantastic!"

None of the other counselors wanted to try it, but Larry shouted back, "How deep is the water down there?"

"Over our heads!" they replied.

"I can't swim in water over my head."

"C'mon, Larry! We'll catch you!"

That was all he needed to hear. He splashed out to the Sliding Rock, ignoring the warning cries of the other three advisors.

Perched on the top, holding tight, he couldn't see the kids below. Would they catch him? He could drown if they didn't. But the excitement and the promise gave him the courage.

"Here I come," he shouted, and let go.

He streaked down the long rock slide, leaning backwards for balance. He felt his shoulder blades bumping against the timeless monolith. His upturned feet directed water spray into his face, and the wind whistled past his ears. Then he plunged into the deep water and paddled frantically to break to the surface again.

He gulped a breath of air and shook the water out of his eyes. A whole circle of kids was waiting for him, beaming at his courage and their shared adventure. They guided him to the side of the natural pool where he could pull himself out, hand over hand, on the waiting rope.

That night he led devotions for the group. He asked someone to read I Corinthians 12:12-27, the much-loved passage describing the Church as the Body of Christ, all parts working together for the common good and for the glory of God. Then Larry said, "Kids, you really made me feel good today, the way all of you helped me have this neat experience. I believe this is one example of what Paul means here in

Corinthians when he talks about the Body of Christ. We're all separate parts, all different, but when we work together, as we did today at Sliding Rock, we have a wonderful time doing more than any one of us could do alone. No way could I have done that without you there to catch me.

"Here in verses 24 to 26, Paul says, 'God has put the body together in such a way that extra honor and care are given to those parts that might otherwise seem less important. This makes for happiness among the parts, so that the parts have the same care for each other that they do for themselves. If one part suffers, all parts suffer with it, and if one part is honored, all the parts are glad.'" [Living Bible]

Larry concluded, "I'm really glad you made it possible for me to have this fantastic experience. We are the Body of Christ, working and playing for God's glory."

The morning of August 4 at the Detroit airport, the Patton family attracts some attention. The parents are middle-aged. Bill, though not tall, is massively built and quiet as a rock. Sandy brown hair tops his flat, round face. His thin lips are a mere slit, and when he speaks, the words come slowly. The liveliest aspect of his features are the barometric blue eyes. While he stands there with his family, those eyes twinkle as Steve, the younger son, cracks a joke to ease tension. Then without turning his head, Bill rolls his eyes at his wife as she asks Larry for the umpteenth time if he's sure he has the name and phone number of the IBM woman in San Jose, just in case. And Bill's eyes fill with proud tears which he sternly refuses to let fall in this public place where Larry is leaving the family nest.

Twenty-one-year-old Steve is dark-haired, tall, wellmuscled, quiet like his dad. His face is unusually kind for one so young. Today he looks down on his older brother and beams with happiness for him. Who would ever have thought that Larry would land a job as a systems engineer with a company like IBM and, even more amazing, be able to fly to California and live on his own! What a miracle!

Sue's prematurely white hair is thick around her narrow face. She and Bill are the same height and both somewhat overweight. She is aggressive, energetic, and capable. She has had to be. And now her fingers ache from sewing Velcro on a dozen new shirts for Larry, her last task to enable him to live independently on the other side of the continent. She stands still. Her plastic-framed glasses slide down her nose as she squints, thinking. Then abruptly she pushes the glasses back into place and the words come out in a torrent. "Don't forget to call us when you get settled tonight. You can call us from Denver, too, if you don't know what else to do with yourself during the layover. I *guess* we'll be home by the time you land in Denver." She glances at Bill for confirmation.

He nods once, pursing his thin lips and winking at Larry.

"Sure, Mom." Larry's voice is high-pitched and soft. He twists his mouth, laboring to shape the fairly intelligible words. His head is tilted to one side. In his three-piece suit of gray pinstripe, with his thin blond hair carefully combed around his face, narrow like his mother's, he looks like a promising young business man of 23. But inside, his stomach is turning and rumbling. He hasn't been able to eat because of nervousness. And his mind is churning, too.

Even though he has the name of the IBM woman in San Jose, he doesn't know who will be meeting his plane. He doesn't know exactly where he is to go, who his boss will be, where he will live. He doesn't know anyone in that part of California. And he doesn't really know how long he will be gone.

On the other hand, all the details of his departure have worked out beautifully. Mom has his new clothes ready, he's had a terrific time on the work camp in North Carolina, and the wedding was wonderful. Someone has even made arrangements to sublet his apartment, so he will have no expenses in Detroit while he is in San Jose. Mom and Dad will pick up his paychecks and deposit them for him, and he will live off his *per diem* in California. Everything is working out fine.

His stomach rumbles, and Mom asks, "Didn't you have breakfast, Larry?"

"No."

"You should have eaten something!" she exclaims.

"I imagine they'll feed him on the plane," Bill puts in.

Steve and Larry look at each other. Mom and Dad can't quit acting like parents, even though Larry is about to take off for the other side of the country and Steve will graduate from University of Michigan in a couple of weeks.

All the luggage is checked through, all the prayers said, and all the questions asked and answered. There is nothing to do but sit and wait.

"Isn't it about time for them to call my flight?" Larry asks querulously. Holding firmly to both arms of the chair and leading with chin thrust out, he pushes himself to his feet and begins to walk to the check-in desk. One arm bends up from the elbow, and his hand folds back at the wrist, the fingers curled. The other arm swings backward in a circular motion. His whole posture seems balanced from the seat of his pants, like a marionette. His lower legs swing out before moving forward. His gait is graceful in an ungainly way. He reaches the counter just as the ticket agent clicks on the intercom.

Seeing Larry there, the man shuts off the microphone and says, "I'm just ready to announce your flight, sir. If you'd like to go ahead and board. . . ."

"No, I'll wait." Larry turns abruptly and rejoins his family.

Once again he has rejected special treatment, determined as always to prove he can function on his own.

"Now boarding wheelchair passengers, escorted children, and First Class passengers at Gate 26 for United's Flight 2047 to Denver. Have your boarding passes ready, please. Tourist Class passengers in one moment."

Bill and Sue blink back tears as they give Larry a final hug. The brothers give a good, hard, thumbs-up handshake, grinning shyly, proudly. Then Larry turns away and joins the line of tourist class passengers at Gate 26. He does not look back. He is ready for Denver, San Jose, IBM, and whatever else his future holds.

Bill, Sue, and Steve hurry to the heavy plate glass wall. The plane throbs with controlled force as the passengers wind through the boarding tube. The Pattons hope for a glimpse of Larry through the small, thick windows of the plane, but they can't see his wave.

One final call for passengers, a brief pause, and then the intravenous tube is retracted from the body of the sleek steel bird that will bear Larry away. His family watches it taxi, turn, roar, then race into flight. It climbs sharply and then is hidden in the haze of the August heat.

"Thank you, God. Go with him," they whisper, staring at the empty sky.

Flying above the country, Larry finds himself recalling the week in North Carolina. By far the best part was the afternoon at Sliding Rock. Now here he is in mid-air, at the top of the slide again, so to speak. Will people "catch" him when he lands in California? Again, the excitement and the promise give him courage. God, working through many people through all these years, has never failed him. And His people are everywhere.

To God be the glory.

Epilogue

People did catch Larry in California, and in no time he was established in an apartment and driving a rental sports car. He found a church home and made new friends quickly.

Although his home office is still Detroit, Larry has travelled frequently for IBM to places like Dallas, Atlanta, Washington, D.C., and New York. In each location he has a group of business friends, many of whom are also committed Christians.

Never one to be left out when friends are having fun, Larry has become a golfer and a skier, first cross-country and, more recently, down-hill skiing. He also enjoys bowling and playing church league softball. He has even taken up photography, by using a tripod and a remote shutter release gadget on an instamatic 35mm. camera.

In gratitude for the help he received early in his schooling, Larry has met with parents of handicapped children, groups like TPOG. He has also spoken to high school classes about what it's like to be a handicapped person and how a person with a handicap would prefer to be treated. He has been invited to speak in churches and in other religious organizations such as Campus Crusade for Christ, and Youth For Christ in several states about how God has worked in his life.

It sounds like a wonderfully exciting, productive life, and

it has been, except for one missing ingredient—someone to share it. One after another, Larry's friends married, and he felt more and more alone. When Steve and Stephanie were wed in the fall of 1981, Larry had the empty feeling that he was losing his brother. His married friends continued to invite him to their homes, but he needed a wife of his own. Was this part of God's plan for him? He dated many women, but none of them wanted to be more than a friend.

Finally he dated Jennifer, a lovely Christian who teaches third grade. Their love for each other developed rapidly, and on June 12, 1987, they were married in a joyous church ceremony celebrated with many friends and relatives.

In 1984 Larry joined a tour of Israel led by Josh McDowell, a Christian speaker and writer whose ministry is based in Dallas. [See Afterword.] As a result, Larry launched a speaking ministry called Hurdling Handicaps. With an advisory board to assist him in planning, he has spoken to various groups in several states.

The church is still a major focal point of his life. He is active in the weekly Men's Prayer Breakfasts, the adult chapter of Fellowship of Christian Athletes, and a young married couples' Bible study group. He is still a member of the First Presbyterian Church of Royal Oak, Michigan.

Both Bill and Sue are now retired from teaching.

Larry or Sue may be contacted by writing to this address:

> Mr. Larry Patton
> or
> Mrs. William Patton
> Hurdling Handicaps
> P.O. Box 725023
> Berkley, MI 48072

Larry receives God and Country Award, June 13, 1971. Larry in Scout uniform and Dick Stratton (far right), who made it possible for Larry to go to D-A Boy Scout camp.

Larry, the "rock hound," in Michigan's upper penninsula, August 1973. David and Lisa Mitchell in background.

Larry and Steve. The taller brother has the advantage here.

Larry practicing basketball. Larry learned to throw and catch a ball by throwing a small rubber hard ball against this garage door. He did this day in and day out for several summers.

Janice and Larry at Larry's home on way to Larry's senior prom, May 1974.

Larry, June 1974, ready for "Royal Oak Kimball High School Graduation."

Camping in Toronto. Larry posed by this IBM sign in July 1979 about the time he went to work full time at IBM.

Larry at General Motors headquarters for an IBM promotion, 1978. "IBM co-op student."

Sue's family at Steve and Stephanie's wedding, October 6, 1981.

25th anniversary party for Sue and Bill. The Rev. Craig Davies (left), the Rev. Robert Miller (right), Steve, Sue, Bill, Larry.

Steve and Stephanie's wedding, October 6, 1981. "Larry is best man for brother Steve."

Dick and Jeni Wiggers, Sue and Bill Patton, Larry in back, at Dick's
ordination, Mobile, Alabama.

Larry (left) and Steve, August 11, 1984, at surprise party for Bill—
"Bill's birthday party."

Larry at Lake Mary near Yosemite National Park.

Josh McDowell and Larry in Israel, 1984.

Larry at 8100′ on top of Sentinel Dome at Yosemite National Park.

Larry gives talk at Campus Crusade Singles Conference, Keystone, Colorado, on Thanksgiving Day, 1986. Jenny and Larry got engaged this day.

Larry, Jenny, Stephanie, Steve, Danny, Grandpa, Grandma, Lisa, Jodie, Mary, and David at Grandma and Grandpa's 60th anniversary, March 1988.

Sue, Bill and Larry after Larry's talk at High School Boys Fellowship of Christian Athletes Camp, Albion, Michigan.

Larry.

Larry, Scenic Drive, California, Summer 1981.

Jenny and Larry's wedding, June 12, 1987.

Jenny and Larry, married June 12, 1987.

Afterword

In November of 1984, I met Larry Patton when he joined our ministry tour to Israel. Larry's courage, determination and true grit gave me an appreciation for him that has only increased over the years. I remember Larry's great enthusiasm in swimming in the Dead Sea, and his perseverance in climbing down Masada in spite of his cerebral palsy. Larry knew no one else in the group at the beginning of the tour, but by the end, everyone had been befriended and touched by this remarkable young man.

Larry had prayed for healing of his handicap many times. I prayed with him for a miracle. A miracle came, but not the one we had expected. Later that week, Larry relinquished himself and his body totally to the Lord. Larry told God that he was willing to have cerebral palsy forever if He could use him more effectively that way.

As I told the tour group on Mount Nebo the five reasons Moses said he could not be used by God, Larry listened intently. One reason Moses believed God couldn't use him was his stuttering. God took Moses, with all his limitations and shortcomings and used him for His glory. God then impressed upon Larry that if he were willing to be used, God could give Larry a clear voice to share the gospel. As an expression of his faith, Larry started a speaking ministry called Hurdling Handicaps.

It's been with great joy that I have seen Larry's ministry flourish. In 1986 and 1987, I invited Larry to speak at a Christian conference on board a cruise ship. The results were stunning. Those who listened were overwhelmed with God's sufficiency in their lives instead of being crippled by their own limitations and shortcomings.

Larry's life is an example of how God can work in extraordinary ways in ordinary people. God took what could have been a negative, defeating, depressing situation and brought about victory. This book relives that story. It will cause you to hurdle your handicap, whether it be one seen on the out-side or known only to you on the inside. *More Than an Average Guy* literally fleshes out Philippians 4:13: "I can do all things through Christ who strengthens me."

Josh McDowell

Index